Building the Sustainable Law Firm

Developing and Implementing an ESG Strategy

Authors
Robert F van Beemen and Sophie Boyer Chammard

Managing director
Sian O'Neill

Building the Sustainable Law Firm: Developing and Implementing an ESG Strategy
is published by

Globe Law and Business Ltd
3 Mylor Close
Horsell
Woking
Surrey GU21 4DD
United Kingdom
Tel: +44 20 3745 4770
www.globelawandbusiness.com

Building the Sustainable Law Firm: Developing and Implementing an ESG Strategy

ISBN 9781787428072
EPUB ISBN 9781787428089
Adobe PDF ISBN 9781787428096

Table of contents

Introduction

Drivers of sustainability come from diverse sources: client demand; lawyers' and employees' expectations; pressure from non-governmental organisations (NGOs); international frameworks and regulations; and input from scientists and experts. Governments cannot act in isolation and companies cannot bear the burden of making our world sustainable on their own; instead, all actors – including corporates, financial players and consumers – must play their part in driving the transition to sustainability.

Law firms are businesses, just like any other. As such, they must be aware of the externalities and hidden costs of their activities, and have a strategy to ensure that their business is sustainable in the long run.

In addition, because of the nature of their advisory activities, law firms must be ready to accompany clients on their own journeys towards sustainability and help them have a positive social impact.

But what's in it for law firms themselves?

The defensive answer is that if they fail to embrace the environmental, social and governance (ESG) agenda, law firms will lose their licence to operate. ESG is not merely a fashion, as some might suggest; it demands a profound transformation of businesses in general. And if law firms do not accept this, they will find themselves unable to assist their clients.

The more proactive answer is that ESG presents new business opportunities and innovative ways of doing business that law firms can capitalise on to gain a competitive advantage in the market. This is what we will attempt to demonstrate in the following pages.

This Special Report looks at the business drivers for sustainability in law firms and offers a practical toolkit to guide firms on their ESG journey. It is essential reading for all lawyers, law firm leaders and management teams who are involved in implementing sustainability strategies at both a firm and practice group level.

Part I: Sustainability and law – setting the scene

Before we make the business case for sustainability (Part II) and present a practical toolkit that will assist your law firm on its journey towards sustainability (Part III), we begin by mapping the context in which law firms operate with regard to sustainability.

First, this report explores key concepts which are not always well understood. It then charts the historic evolution of the regulatory landscape, which makes lawyers uniquely placed to help clients navigate the expanding maze of complex regulations.

In this evolving context, how are law firms, as businesses, adapting? More often reactively, in response to client demand, which creates a 'trickle-down effect'; but sometimes progressively. We discuss the different ages of corporate responsibility to highlight how the journey towards sustainability is an ongoing one.

And law firms are not on their own on this journey. Some law societies and bar associations are encouraging law firms to engage in ESG. Increasingly, legal community associations are taking clear positions to assist their members. And a growing number of coalitions between major firms and businesses are making ambitious collective moves.

The message is clear: law firms must reconsider – and are

reconsidering – the way they do business in order to help preserve the environment and society. Like all other businesses, they should follow the global framework of the United Nations Sustainable Development Goals (SDGs) as the most accurate and useful compass when embarking on their sustainability journey.

The first part of this Special Report sets the context through a discussion of the following:

- key definitions;
- history and the developing body of rules;
- law firms' growing awareness of sustainability; and
- the SDGs as the universal compass for ESG in law firms.

1. Definitions: 'corporate social responsibility', 'sustainable development' or 'ESG'?

These terms – often overused and sometimes used out of context or as mere 'tick-the-box' expressions – require clear definition as used in this Special Report.

1.1 Corporate social responsibility

Corporate social responsibility (CSR) is the voluntary commitment of businesses to operate in a responsible way and contribute a net positive impact to society and the environment. Companies often have a dedicated CSR department and base their efforts on established norms or guiding principles (eg, ISO 26000; the Global Compact; the Organisation for Economic Co-operation and Development principles), to ensure that processes are in place to manage their business responsibly.

1.2 'Sustainability' or 'sustainable development'

'Sustainability' is a broader term. It refers to a comprehensive systemic approach whereby a business considers all its stakeholders and adapts its business model to create and share value both for immediate shareholders and for society and the planet. The level of engagement is stronger, as it is part of a wider undertaking to position the business within a global sustainable system. Society at large is placed at the centre of the business's strategy, governance and purpose. The growth of a sustainable business does not compromise, but rather positively impacts on society and the environment. For a business, sustainability encompasses everything from finance to supply chains, product development and production, and business model. Sustainable development results in growth and profits, as well as positive impacts that outweigh the negative impacts on society and the environment.

"For a business, sustainability encompasses everything from finance to supply chains, product development and production, and business model."

1.3 ESG criteria

ESG criteria are the main factors or key performance indicators (KPIs) used by investors when considering responsible investment in businesses. ESG criteria are now analysed with regard to the SDGs (explained in detail in Part I, section 4):

- **Environmental sustainability** relates to how a business performs as a steward of the natural environment, focusing on waste and pollution, oceans, essential resources, water, erosion of biodiversity, land use and deforestation, ozone depletion, carbon emissions and climate change.
- **Social responsibility** concerns how a company treats people and encompasses employee relations, diversity, working conditions – including child labour and slavery – and health and safety both in the workplace and in the supply chain. Another important aspect of social responsibility concerns wider societal responsibility towards local communities in the places where the company operates.
- **Governance** covers how a corporation polices itself – how it is governed – and focuses on the letter and spirit of its decision-making processes, its tax strategy, executive remuneration, anti-corruption and anti-bribery policies, and the diversity of the management board.

2. Sustainability: from slow raising of awareness to exponential growth of regulations

In the 1970s, scientists began raising awareness of the damage that human activity was causing to the environment and to the climate. Society and NGOs have since become increasingly vocal in criticising traditional ways of doing business, insisting that businesses should take account of their negative impact on society and the environment.

International organisations have developed a complex body of indicative guidelines and rules over the past 50 years. Increasingly, these rules are becoming binding regulations which seek to encourage corporates to conduct their business in a sustainable way. Their scope is incredibly broad, encompassing all aspects of business management and strategy. And more regulations are being introduced all around the world.

While many of these regulations are not binding on most law firms – either because they fall below the legal thresholds or because their legal status (where they are not commercial companies) is not yet covered by them – it seems clear that firms will be brought within their scope sooner or later. Law firms would thus be well advised to start thinking now about the relevant issues, as the sooner they do so, the easier it will be for them to embark on their ESG journey.

Let's start with the historical evolution that has seen this tsunami of rules develop.

2.1 From research and scientists ...

Research shows that human activity has caused serious damage to the environment since the industrial revolution. The first major reference study to be published was the Meadows Report[1] in 1972. It revealed, through computer simulations, the correlation between economic development and population growth in a world with finite resources, and demonstrated that there are social and environmental limits to growth. This prompted extensive debate, research and conferences around the world.

Over the past decade, more studies – including the latest report of the Intergovernmental Panel on Climate Change[2] (IPCC) – have confirmed that if we continue with our current focus on economic, industrial and population growth, this will have a negative – perhaps even irreversible – impact on the climate, biodiversity and the environment, which in turn will increase inequalities and severe poverty.

2.2 ... to increasing pressure from society ...

First coined in the 1950s, the terminology of CSR[3] developed after the first oil shock, as society began to criticise traditional business increasingly harshly for not respecting the common good or society at large.

In 1984, the 'shareholder value' theory was challenged by the 'stakeholder value' theory[4] – that is, businesses should create value not only for their direct shareholders, but also for their employees, the value chain, clients and neighbourhoods. While the contribution that business makes to increasing living standards is recognised, society criticises those business which are greedy for profits or which lack ethics.

In recent decades, pressure from citizens, NGOs (eg, climate activist marches), consumers (eg, the anti-black Friday movement, ethical fashion) and investors has increased significantly, leading to the dawn of socially responsible investing.

2.3 ... to voluntary responsibility of businesses

It is mainly due to this pressure from society that businesses voluntarily began to establish CSR departments and take appropriate action.

These initial efforts were encouraged and guided by international organisations, which prepared recommendations and principles to harmonise behaviours through 'soft law'.

2.4 From soft law and the need for guidelines ...

Over the past 50 years, international organisations such as the United Nations, the International Labour Organisation and the World Economic Forum have revealed the negative impact of our pace and means of development on people and the planet. Increasing numbers of non-binding rules, recommendations and principles encourage states, businesses and civil society to adopt sustainable behaviour.

The timeline in Figure 1 (overleaf) provides a very quick overview of the historical development of these regulations, which began with indicative norms.

Over the past 20 years, sustainability has become a key topic in international conventions, as studies have highlighted the increased urgency of progress in this sphere.

These principles and guidelines aim to support and promote the transformation of companies towards social responsibility; and while initially they were primarily non-binding, they are increasingly being underpinned by binding regulations.

2.5 ... to binding regulations and hard law

A few major guidelines and international frameworks have binding effect, while others have inspired binding laws. Figure 2 (on page 15) provides examples of important international treaties which are binding for member states, a game-changing EU directive and a focus on French national laws.

Figure 1. Selected milestones to the development of sustainability: the power of soft law[5]

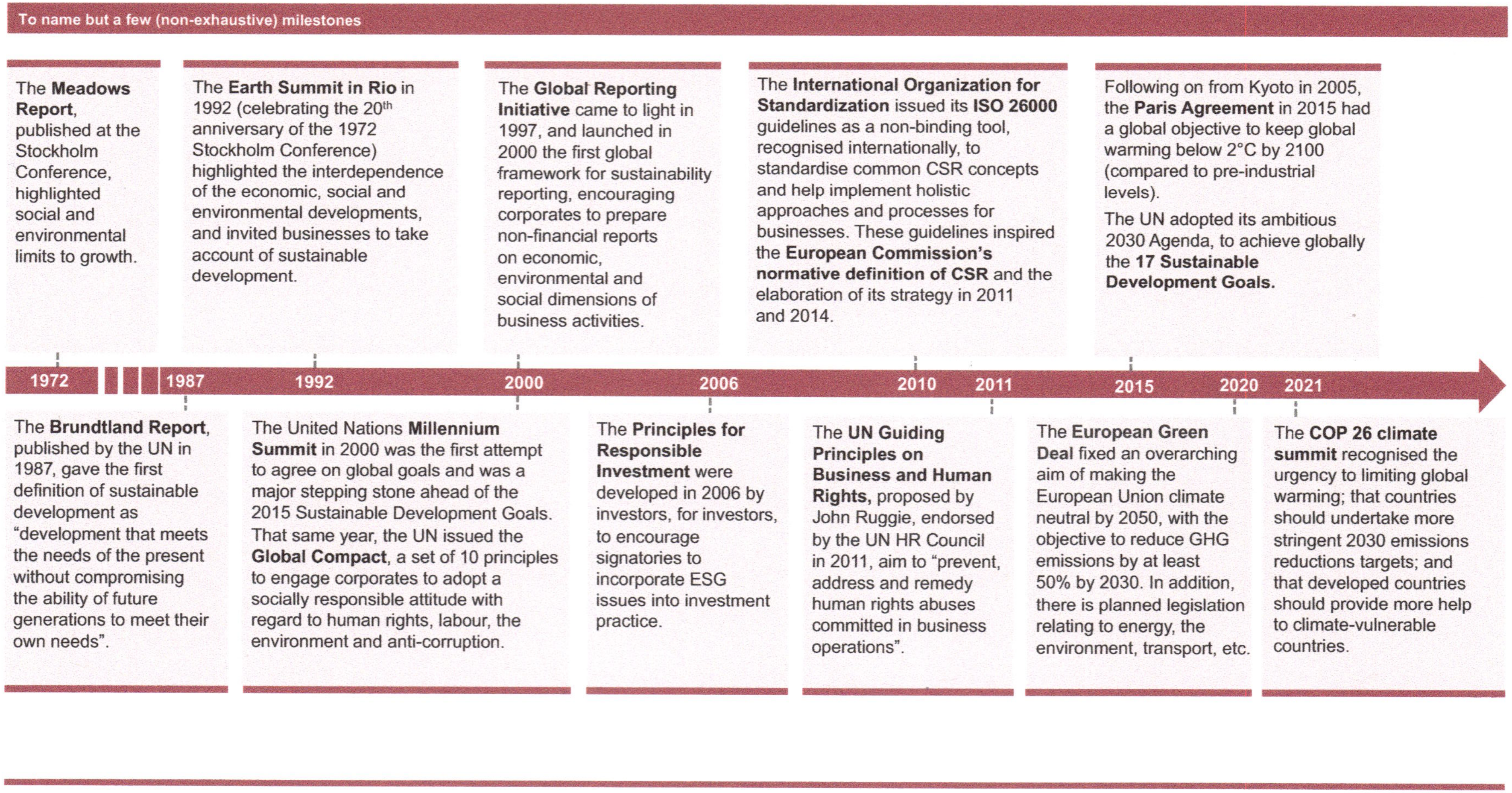

Source: Venturis Consulting Group, all rights reserved.

Figure 2. Examples of binding regulations

International treaties

The **International Labour Organization** (ILO) established universal labour rights in 1998 in its Declaration of Fundamental Principles and Rights at Work, including the right to unionise and the prohibition of forced labour, child work and discrimination.

The **OECD Guidelines for Multinational Enterprises** required each member state to appoint National Contact Points for Responsible Business Conduct, with the objective to engage businesses in applying its guidelines and progress in sustainability.

EU directives

The **Non-Financial Reporting Directive (NFRD)** (2014/95/EU):
A game changer, requiring large companies to provide an extra-financial annual report for stakeholders on their social and environmental impact, protection of human rights and anti-corruption measures. The report is mandatory for "large companies of public interest" and if they have more than 500 employees. Member states can be more demanding.
The NFRD will be followed by other EU initiatives to meet the Green Deal objectives, such as:

- the Corporate Sustainability Reporting Directive (CSRD), aiming to replace and strengthen the NFRD, applicable in 2024 (for 2023 reports); and
- the EU Taxonomy Regulation, a classification tool to define and guide investors on which activities are sustainable.

National laws

France is an interesting example where the legislator has sometimes been a precursor.
For instance:

- Loi Sapin II 2016 creates a duty of vigilance extended to the business's entire supply chain.
- Loi PACTE 2019 includes sustainability at three levels:
  - All companies must take account of their social and environmental challenges.
  - Companies can include a 'purpose' in their by-laws (next to their object) as a stronger and more visible commitment with regard to their responsibility.
  - Companies may opt to become a '*société à mission*' (mission corporation audited by an independent third party).

Source: Venturis Consulting Group, all rights reserved.

Overall, sustainability is now the subject of a tsunami of regulations with different scope and effect. Lawyers are ideally placed to navigate this complex area of the law and thus to assist their clients (more on this in Part II).

But to what extent are law firms themselves subject to these rules? Law firms are business actors and, like any other business, are encouraged to act sustainably, whatever their form or size. For some legal obligations, such as the EU Non-financial Reporting Directive,[6] the regulators initially focused on large companies (including some large law firms established as limited liability partnerships (LLPs) in the United Kingdom). However, their scope of application is gradually expanding. The overarching message is that all actors – including individuals and small to medium-sized firms – have a role to play. International Organization for Standardization (ISO) norms and the SDGs are aimed at all economic actors, regardless of status or size.

To conclude this discussion of the development of sustainability regulations, what started out as non-binding principles not only have evolved into an increasing number of international legally binding obligations for governments and corporates, but also – perhaps even more importantly – have created a deep sense of awareness of the importance of sustainability for all actors in society, from governments to consumers, businesses and law firms.

3. Law firms: towards proactive engagement in the sustainability journey

Professional service providers such as law firms have special roles and responsibilities in (international) business. With their expertise, know-how and capabilities, they act as the lubricant of the legal, tax and accountancy infrastructure on which (international) business is based.

As the regulatory rules of the game continue to evolve towards sustainability, lawyers have become instrumental in facilitating their clients' journey. Initially, law firms were required to engage in ESG due to client needs. They are now themselves climbing the ladder of the different stages of CSR.

3.1 Reactive law firms and the 'trickle-down effect'

Although law firms are not frontrunners in terms of sustainability, they have become increasingly aware of their special roles and responsibilities.

When it comes to sustainability, law firms would be best described as 'reactive'.[7] The trickle-down effect chart in Figure 3 depicts how most law firms get involved.

Figure 3. The trickle-down effect

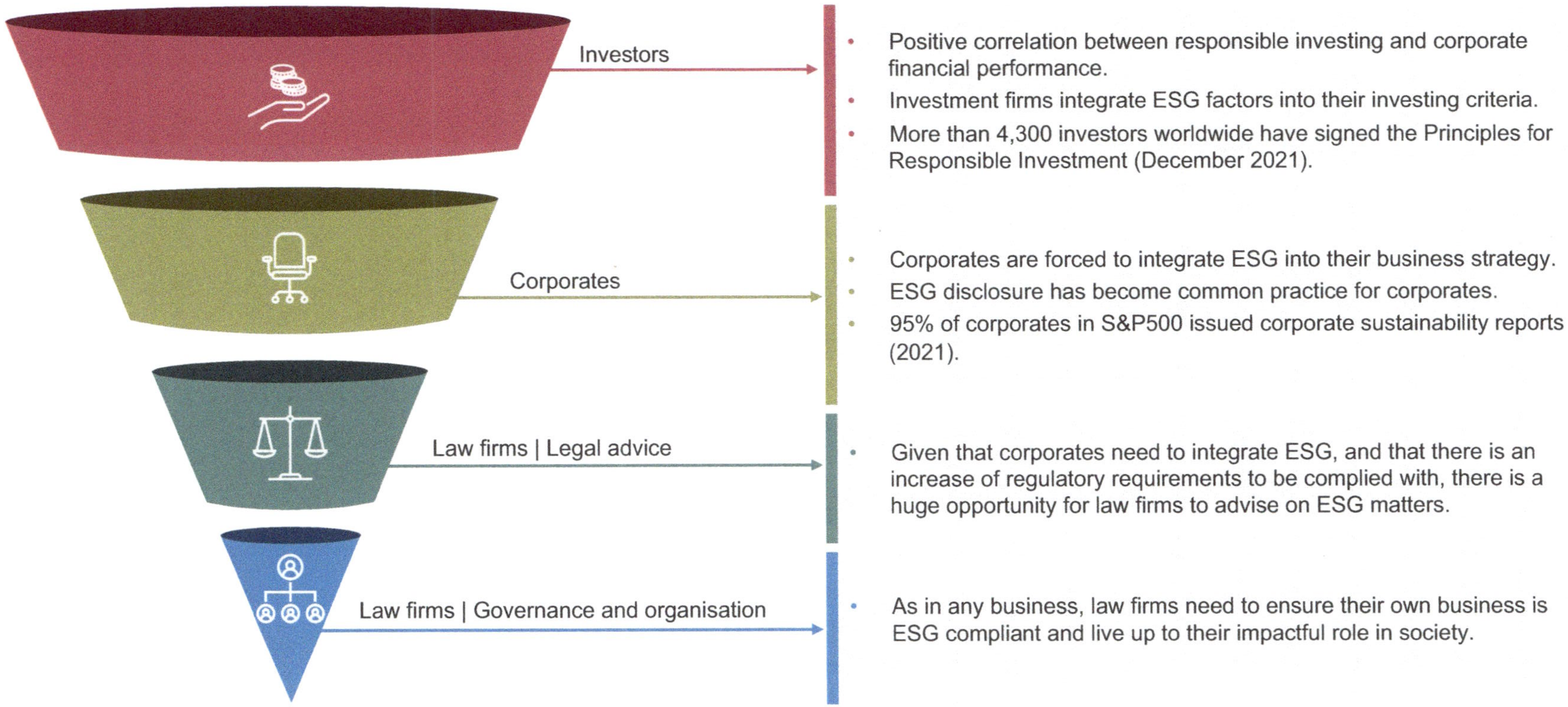

Source: Venturis Consulting Group, all rights reserved.

Driven by financial performance and societal pressure, investment firms are increasingly integrating ESG factors into their investment criteria.[8] Consequently, corporates are forced by their shareholders (ie, investment funds) to integrate ESG into their corporate strategies.[9] They are further encouraged to do so by consumer behaviour, growing activist action and new norms and regulations.

These developments require legal service providers to have a profound understanding of the ESG threats, opportunities and challenges that lie ahead.

Law firms have a vital role to play on this journey – first, as legal advisers in guiding their clients through their ESG transformation (see more in Part II, section 3); and second, as independent business actors in their own right.

As awareness of sustainability grows, law firms are now starting out on their own journeys. It is worth pausing here to identify where a firm sits along the different stages of sustainability engagement, to assess how best to move forward.

3.2 The different economic ages of social responsibility within a law firm

Law firms, like all other businesses, pass through different stages on their corporate responsibility journeys. Drawing an analogy to the 'Ages of Responsibility' model described by Wayne Visser (see Figure 4 on page 21),[10] it is worth determining what stage a law firm is at in terms of sustainability and assessing the level of transformation that the law firm needs to achieve.

(a) The 'greed age'

In the 'greed age', a firm is primarily focused on benefiting its partners and lawyers, and takes a defensive approach to responsibility – that is, it will consider CSR issues only if it is legally bound by them or if it needs to obtain financing.

(b) The 'philanthropy age'

Most firms are in the 'philanthropy age', when they set aside a share of their profits to give funds to (or raise funds for) a charitable cause, in the form of gifts, donations or sponsorships.

Such causes may be cultural: for example, a law firm may sponsor a gallery and take the opportunity to invite clients and/or employees to an exhibition in order to strengthen relationships outside daily business. Other causes may be fully altruistic, linked to access to justice, health or the eradication of poverty.

Some law firms have established foundations to fund and manage several charitable causes. Often linked to tax credits and aimed at attracting positive publicity, foundations are a good management and incentive method to benefit society generously while also bringing some value to the firm.[11]

Pro bono legal assistance is another important way for most law firms to contribute to society. It has been a longstanding tradition for law firms to provide *pro bono* legal services or defend people who otherwise could not pay for the services of a lawyer.

In the United States, firms have been more committed to practising and publicising their *pro bono* services than in continental Europe, where *pro bono* services have traditionally more often depended on discrete individual generosity and have not been organised as a structured firm service. This is probably due to cultural reasons: in continental Europe, state social benefits ensure access to social security and legal aid for those who would not otherwise benefit from these services; while in the United States, a more liberal culture with few state benefits requires private firms to step in. However, these differences have become less distinct over time and all law firms would now appear to be in some sort of philanthropic or marketing age (see below).

(c) The 'marketing age'

In the 'marketing age', law firms ensure that their actions can be marketed and communicated – sometimes to the extent that they are used as a PR or promotion tool. Given the propensity of NGOs and the public to lobby against companies which do not contribute positively to society or the environment, communicating what a firm does in this regard is a no brainer. However, a firm must draw the line between transparent communication, which explains its contribution truly and honestly, and what is generally called 'greenwashing' – that is, communicating on specific actions with no effort to fundamentally change its business model.

(d) The 'management age'

As yet, few law firms have transitioned to the 'management age'. Those firms which have done so have embraced social responsibility and are ensuring that they comply with general principles and satisfy the interests of both partners and society at large. Various charts and codes of conduct will be signed within the firm to ensure that employees take ESG seriously and take account of their supply chain. Incremental improvements are made – albeit rarely with the right scope and urgency.

(e) The 'sustainability age'

The final stage is that of the sustainable law firm, which thinks in a more systemic way and considers changing its business model (ie, the way in which it generates revenues and profits). These firms can become innovative in the services they offer or in how they work to ensure that they offer the best value to clients, while at the same time sharing work with other suppliers (eg, alternative legal service providers, independent lawyers) to achieve the greatest possible efficiencies, ensure that associates learn and develop their capabilities and skills, and generate profits for the partners.

This discussion of the different stages highlights that sustainability is a journey. Most law firms have already embarked on this journey, whatever their reasons and whatever their specific initiatives or programmes. All stages are valuable steps in progressing towards the achievement of the SDGs.

3.3 More support from legal market institutions and actions from leaders

Individual law firms are not alone on this journey. Legal sector institutions are increasingly conscious of the need for their guidance. Law societies and legal associations sometimes set the tone and share best practices and guidance with their members.

It is worth considering legal institutions' own journeys towards sustainability. They too are walking this path: some are setting the tone and trying to be role models or issuing guidelines for members, while others lag behind; but awareness is growing.

Set out below are some indicative snapshots of collective efforts at different levels in the profession. National legal market institutions (law societies and bar associations), international associations and collectives of leading international firms are all acting at different levels to lead the way.

(a) National bar institutions and law societies paving the way

National professional associations have very different approaches, from no involvement at all to being quite sustainability conscious and providing support for their members.

Figure 5 (on page 22) presents examples of active legal institutions.

(b) Legal associations spreading the word

International legal associations have embraced sustainability as a central issue (see Figure 6 on page 24). Hardly a day goes by without a seminar or workshop inviting lawyers to discuss CSR, sustainability, gender diversity or diversity and inclusion (D&I) more generally, as well as human rights and ethical rules.

Figure 4. The ages and stages of CSR

Economic age	Stage of CSR	*Modus operandi*	Key enabler	Stakeholder target
Greed	Defensive	*Ad hoc* interventions	Investments	Shareholders, government and employees
Philanthropy	Charitable	Charitable programmes	Projects	Communities
Marketing	Promotional	Public relations	Media	General public
Management	Strategic	Management systems	Codes	Shareholders and NGOs/CSOs
Sustainability	Systemic	Business models	Services	Regulators, clients, collaborations

Source: Based on Wayne Visser, "The Age of Responsibility: CSR 2.0 and the New DNA of Business" (see n 10).

Figure 5. Examples of legal institutions leading the way

The Law Society of England and Wales

- Published in October 2021 a "climate change resolution showing the role lawyers can play in addressing the climate crisis", undertaking to support solicitors and urging them to engage.
- Has a policy for diversity and inclusion, with a Diversity Access Scheme "supporting talented solicitors from less privileged backgrounds" with mentoring, work experience and funds.
- Commits to, and incites its members to, sign the Diversity and Inclusion Charter (established in 2009).
- Created a social mobility ambassadors scheme.
- Committed in June 2019 to creating "a more equal legal profession for all" and offers toolkits to promote 'Women in Leadership in Law'.
- Facilitates *pro bono* initiatives and access to justice via its Law Society Charity.
- …

Paris Bar

- Supports the UN Global Compact.
- Assessed according to the ISO 26000 standard guidelines in 2013.
- Produces annual CSR report based on the ISO 26000 standard referential.
- Offered to share the cost of ISO 26000 evaluation, with law firms who entered into an ISO 26000 process; VIGO was the first law firm to benefit from the offer.
- Encourages its members to sign its "Charter of the responsible lawyer".
- Obtained the Gender Equality Label, and was rated 95/100 by the Gender Equality Index.
- Has established a longstanding and active *pro bono* organisation and an endowment fund, *Barreau de Paris Solidarité*, to engage lawyers in and fund *pro bono* projects.
- …

French National Bar Council

- Issued in 2011 a useful questionnaire and guidelines for law firms to think about sustainability.
- Issued a charter for "Social responsibility of law firms".
- …

Source: Venturis Consulting Group, all rights reserved.

(c) Market-leading collaborative approaches

Figure 7 (on page 25) sets out three important joint initiatives of lawyers and coalitions of legal market-leading firms[12] aimed at reducing carbon emissions and achieving net zero. In rising to this global challenge, collaborations towards these goals are much more powerful than individual action alone.

While awareness of sustainability is growing within the legal sector, and law firms are still at very different stages of their journey, regulatory bodies, international legal associations and coalitions of market leaders are helping to design paths for them to embark and progress on this journey.

The trends are clear and irreversible. Sustainability is no longer a 'nice to have', but a 'must have' – not only because it is a good way of doing business, but also because it enables firms to be competitive and profitable while simultaneously benefiting both the environment and society.

The legal sector is on its way towards sustainability, albeit with players moving at different paces. But it is undeniable that law firms must now set their own objectives to achieve sustainability. In doing so, they should turn to the most comprehensive, most helpful and most commonly used compass to navigate sustainability: the SDGs.

4. The Sustainable Development Goals: a universal compass for businesses and law firms

The SDGs are guiding the formulation and development of sustainability strategies both by corporates and, increasingly, by law firms. The 2030 Agenda of the United Nations is the first programme for sustainable development to set out a concrete plan and engage governments, businesses and civil populations in achieving the SDGs by 2030. The SDGs are the result of a large-scale mobilisation of experts, consulted from all sectors and countries, and provide the best possible framework for law firms to engage in sustainable development, increase access to justice for all and more.

In total, the United Nations sets 17 goals[13] and 169 sub-goals. They are all interrelated. Actors can select and focus on those goals towards which they can have the greatest impact, considering their activity. They may need to do trade-offs and prioritise certain themes or actions to achieve more impactful results.

As the SDGs are the most inspiring, universal and commonly embraced reference and compass towards sustainable development, we would naturally encourage all law firms to commit to them.

Figure 6. Two examples of leading international legal market associations spreading the word

The International Bar Association (IBA)

For the IBA, sustainability is at its core. Established in 1947, the IBA was born under the conviction that it could contribute to global stability and peace through the administration of justice.

- 2015: Adopted the Business and Human Rights Guidance for Bar Associations
- 2016: Practical Guide on Business and Human Rights for Business Lawyers
- 2021: Sustainable Law in Action podcast series, including a conversation with Professor Ruggie, instrumental to the Global Compact and, later, to the UN Guiding Principles of Business and Human Rights
- IBA Human Rights Institute
- IBA Diversity and Inclusion Council and policy
- ESG working group
- ...

The International Association of Young Lawyers (AIJA)

AIJA is a global association for young lawyers and in-house counsel (age <45).

Since 1962 AIJA has provided international opportunities for young lawyers to network, learn and develop.

- In 2020 it published the report "Sustainability is the future of law: A vision for the legal profession".
- The Human Rights Committee of AIJA, through the SOS Avocats programme, supports the right of every lawyer to practise their profession freely and the entitlement of every individual to legal representation, a fair trial and the protection of the rule of law.
- AIJA has dedicated officers in the fields of diversity and sustainability.
- 50% of the senior leadership roles of AIJA are held by women.
- Launched a series of webinars on ESG, "Toolkit for Change" – The Journey Towards a Sustainable Law Firm (2022).
- ...

Source: Venturis Consulting Group, all rights reserved.

Figure 7. Three examples of collective efforts from legal market actors

Legal Sustainability Alliance (LSA)	Chancery Lane Project	Net Zero Lawyers Alliance
The LSA is an alliance for law firms and the legal sector in the UK with the objective to take sustainability forward. Members: • share best practice; • undertake to reduce their carbon footprint; and • share a tool to help calculate and follow carbon emissions. Being a member does not provide certification; nor is data reviewed by third-party experts. Firms are at different stages of their sustainability journey, but all agree to move in the right direction.	This is a project in which many legal professionals collaborate* to draft and share (free of charge) contractual clauses, glossaries and model laws that help fight climate change. It launched the Net Zero Toolkit in 2021, enabling lawyers to use climate and net zero-aligned clauses and tools. This is a special collaboration between volunteering lawyers, where lawyers can have an important influencer role to help corporates pursue their transition to sustainability.	The Net Zero Lawyers Alliance was founded by 20 leading law firms in June 2021, with a view to accelerating the 'Race to Zero'. Founders include HBS, Clifford Chance, Slaughter and May, Baker McKenzie, Arthur Cox, Bates Wells, Shearman & Sterling, Burges Salmon and Eversheds. All signatories undertake the same obligations to comply with the Paris Agreement and they commit to: • engage with their clients' transition; and • implement training and *pro bono* targets throughout the firm.

Source: Venturis Consulting Group, all rights reserved.

* 2,300 as at April 2022.

Most international law firms select a few SDGs to focus on in their sustainability strategy.[14] The most popular in the legal sectors are SDGs 4, 5, 8, 10, 13, 16 and 17. Law firms also refer to many more of the SDGs, but we have deliberately decided to concentrate on those which are most commonly chosen. In Part III, we will highlight the importance of choosing a select range of these objectives – those where the firm can have the greatest positive impact, which are most important to it, which can make a real difference for stakeholders and for which improvement can be measured.

Let's take a closer look at the most relevant SDGs and the business drivers for the legal sector.[15]

4.1 Peace, justice and strong institutions: SDG 16

Among the priorities most commonly selected by law firms is Goal 16, which relates to their core business. Law firms are best placed to help provide "access to justice for all" and to build "effective, accountable institutions at all levels".[16]

There are numerous examples of lawyers offering *pro bono* services to provide access to justice, preserve the human rights of refugees or defend the freedom of speech of journalists, to name but a few.

"There are numerous examples of lawyers offering pro bono services to provide access to justice, preserve the human rights of refugees or defend the freedom of speech of journalists."

Figure 8. United Nations Sustainable Development Goals

Source: United Nations Sustainable Development Goals (see n 13).

In its annual ESG report for 2019, White & Case claimed that it was focusing mainly on Goal 16, with 57% of its actions dedicated to this end.[17]

However, one challenge in this regard is matching the legal needs of the poorest populations with law firms that have the capacity to offer *pro bono* services. Several NGOs and institutions act as brokers to assist associations that they have screened and whose legal needs they have assessed. For example, A4ID: Advocates for International Development, a global charity based in the United Kingdom, acts as a facilitator, matching the legal needs of the poorest people to the capabilities of international lawyers.[18] Major law firms are working in partnership with this charity to direct their actions.

National institutions are also facilitating the joint efforts of individual lawyers. For example, the Paris Bar's *Bus du Droit* travels to the most deprived Parisian suburbs to provide free legal assistance.[19]

Law firms contribute further to the achievement of Goal 16 when they help build a corpus of laws and clauses, as The Chancery Lane Project[20] is doing to help fight climate change.

4.2 Gender equality and reduced inequalities: SDGs 5 and 10

While access to justice is one obvious area in which law firms can have a major impact, gender equality is another goal on which law firms are increasingly focusing.

"Gender equality is not only a fundamental human right, but a necessary foundation for a peaceful, prosperous, and sustainable world."[21]

There is a general awareness among law firms in developed countries that this objective is key, both within their own organisations and for their external stakeholders and the wider world.

Many law firms have singled out this issue on their websites and in their organisations. Awareness is high. Internally, diversity journeys began in law firms around 20 years ago and are now pursued at different paces, often with the stated objective of having more women represented at partnership level (see further Part II, sections 4 and 5 on talent and leadership).

Externally, law firms often choose to focus on key issues in their *pro bono* programmes, such as women's protection from violence or women's education and work in countries where their basic rights are not sufficiently protected.

"To reduce inequalities, policies should be universal in principle, paying attention to the needs of disadvantaged and marginalised populations."[22]

Most law firms also emphasise this goal and have launched initiatives aimed at improving D&I internally (eg, ethnic; lesbian, gay, bisexual, trans and intersex (LGBTI+); disability), as well as promoting equal rights in their communities and through *pro bono* programmes.

4.3 Quality education and decent work: SDGs 4 and 8

"Obtaining a quality education is the foundation to improving people's lives and sustainable development."[23]

Quality education helps people to climb the socio-economic ladder and access quality jobs. These goals are also linked to gender diversity, as women suffer more frequently from a lack of education or unemployment.

To qualify in the legal profession, a certain level of education is needed. And it is part of the daily job of a lawyer to educate – both clients and associates. When providing legal advice, a lawyer must explain, contextualise and persuade. Therefore, law firms frequently

"Diversity journeys began in law firms around 20 years ago and are now pursued at different paces, often with the stated objective of having more women represented at partnership level."

select SDG 4 on education, as they can make a significant contribution towards its achievement.

The initiatives in this regard are so numerous that merely providing a few examples here would not do them sufficient justice. However, they include a French initiative where lawyers volunteer to teach law to teenagers at schools in underprivileged regions;[24] and law firm fundraising efforts for Barefoot College,[25] which trains Indian women to provide their villages with solar energy.

4.4 Climate action: SDG 13

Climate change is a global challenge that involves everyone, everywhere. However, some lawyers would argue that as law firms are part of the service sector, they are not well placed to make a significant impact towards climate action.

But the situation is so urgent that every economic actor needs to reduce its negative impact on the climate and aim for carbon neutrality. As we will see in Part II, section 6, there is significant room for improvement, whether through building green offices, limiting energy consumption and travelling, or avoiding waste or recycling.

Just before the COP26 conference in 2021,[26] a coalition of more than

20 global firms officialised their undertaking to become net zero by 2050 based on the science-based targets set out in the Paris Agreement.[27]

However, where law firms can have the greatest impact here is in their advice to their clients (see further Part II, section 3).

4.5 Partnerships: SDG 17

In SDG 17, the UN exhorts economic actors to "Revitalise the global partnership for sustainable development".[28] None of the SDGs can be achieved by single actors, sectors, governments, regulators, businesses or consumers alone; sustainability requires a systemic and global approach. Everyone –from the private sector (business) to civil society (consumers), governments, regulators and NGOs – must be involved and committed to reducing their negative impact. And much more can be achieved if each actor calls on the capabilities of others to collaborate accordingly.

(a) Collaboration results in greater and longer-term shared value

It is interesting to see that as early as 2009 – well before the SDGs were introduced in their current form – McKinsey highlighted the importance of partnerships in an impactful graphic (see Figure 9 opposite).[29] When considering the objectives of benefiting both business and society, creating shared value and facilitating substantial improvement, the value achieved through smart partnerships proves a gamechanger.

For law firms, this graph translates easily. 'Pet projects' are small initiatives, undertaken mostly thanks to the energy of a partner and linked to his or her personal interests. This is a good way to start, but such initiatives are unlikely to last or grow beyond that partner's individual investment, and the benefits are likely to be minimal both for the firm and for society. Next come projects that involve more people internally; but the right equilibrium must be found for these to succeed. Purely philanthropic projects primarily benefit society and are unsustainable in the long run. Pure propaganda is aimed more at building the firm's reputation than at creating value for society.

However, partnerships have significant potential to create value over a longer timeframe, both for the firm and for society. This is because they involve more constituents; and because their objectives and benefits are better articulated and can be more ambitious. "All alone we go faster; together we go further," says a wise African proverb. We will discuss the key ingredients for a successful partnership in Part III.

Practically, we like this very simple framework, as it enables firms to map their CSR initiatives and select those that provide long-term value both for business and for society.

Figure 9. Corporate social responsibility: the landscape

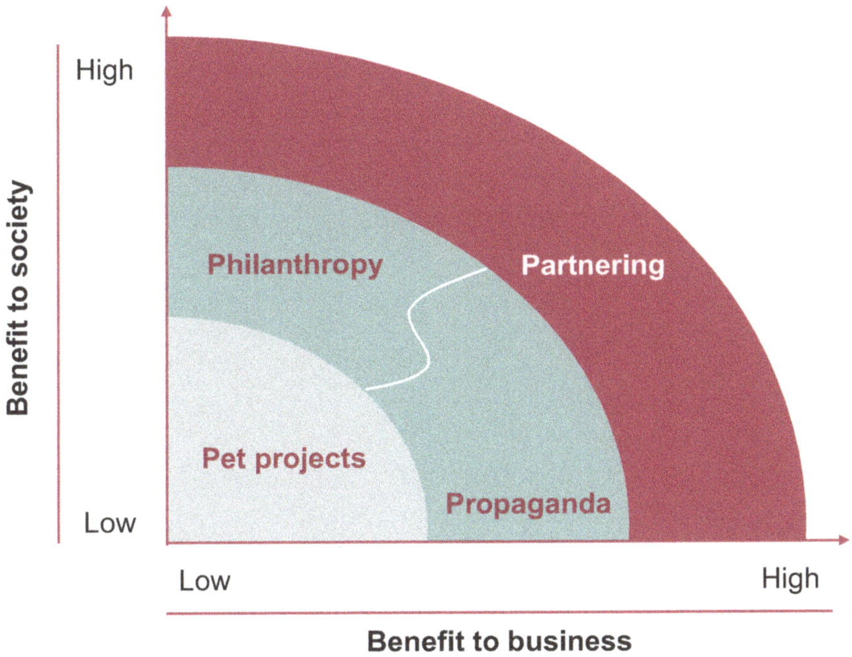

Source: Adapted from Keys, Malnight and van der Graf (see n 29).

(b) Wide range of partnerships for sustainability in the legal sector

A quick scan of sustainability initiatives in the legal sector shows that law firms already have recourse to a wide range of partnership forms, with different objectives. They include the following:

- Individual law firms are teaming up through sectoral coalitions, such as the recently established Net Zero Lawyers Alliance mentioned earlier. The founders include more than 20 global law firms, which are normally direct competitors but have positioned themselves as collaborators on this global issue, "where we'll either all win or all lose".[30]
- Collaborations between lawyers and policy makers, such as the Chancery Lane Project, gather lawyers from around the world to draft new model laws or clauses intended to inspire lawyers and policy makers when advising clients and creating new policies for net zero.[31]
- Another type of collaboration is with clients, accompanying them on the transition to sustainability. Sustainability is now at the top of the agenda for general counsel, who need their external lawyers not only to flag risks, but also to be enablers and collaborators in finding innovative paths forward and

providing solutions. We see more partnerships between clients, tech start-ups and law firms to provide advanced levels of service for each task, generate the best value for clients and share the benefits in the best interests of all parties involved.
- Other opportunities for collaboration arise between law firms and their supply chains. Lawyers are ideally placed to help suppliers identify human rights risks and protect against them.

Innumerable productive partnerships have been forged, such as the following:

- Great examples of broad partnerships that benefit society include:
  - TrustLaw, the Thomson Reuters Foundation's global *pro bono* service;[32] and
  - Dentons' internal Nextlaw Referral Network for all lawyers looking for *pro bono* opportunities.[33]
- Clifford Chance has made collaboration an important axis of its strategy. It has committed to work in partnership with organisations to help achieve the SDGs and has launched the CC SDGs award for NGOs that focus on the environmental SDGs.[34] The prize is a financial donation and *pro bono* hours. The firm has increased its impact by empowering more expert NGOs dedicated to these issues.
- HL Base[35] is Hogan Lovells's social enterprise and social finance practice, which collaborates with Ashoka and UnLTd to provide legal advice to social enterprises. Every young lawyer joining the firm (whether in London, New York, Hong Kong or continental Europe) is invited to complete a mini-MBA course with the practical task of advising a social enterprise on all aspects of its growth (under the supervision of partners and trainers). While receiving this qualitative training, lawyers become familiar with the importance of social impact throughout their activities and are inspired from their earliest days at the firm. In turn, a culture of sustainability is promoted and embedded across the firm.

These examples of collaboration are sustainable, as they considerably increase the value both to law firms and to their constituents, their collaborating partners and society at large. They also illustrate the incredible power of the SDGs, to which we would encourage all businesses to refer directly.

The purpose of this section is to put sustainability into context in the legal sector. For some readers, sustainability may be a rather new topic which has suddenly hit the front pages, whether because of recent disasters and the effects of climate change or because of COP26. But for many law firms, ESG is already at the top of the board's agenda. No firm has as yet realised its objectives; but while the pace and speed may be different, most are on their way, as firms engage both themselves and their employees, clients and suppliers in helping to achieve the SDGs.

For those law firms that have not yet started on this journey, it is time to make the business case for sustainability (Part II). We will then suggest concrete steps for law firms to embark on this journey (Part III).

Part II: The business case for sustainability in law firms

1. Introduction: sustainability as a competitive edge

This Special Report does not discuss how law firms could organise philanthropic programmes or communicate their charitable efforts more efficiently to the market. It rather aims to make sustainability the core of a firm's strategy and positioning, embedded in its culture, client service, talent management, governance and processes. It will attempt to convince partners that sustainability is not just about good intentions, but about putting the benefits at the centre of the firm's business model in a way that yields benefits to the partners, as well as to the wider stakeholders of the firm.

Firms that have a culture of sustainability are financially more successful for their partners, while also providing benefits to the environment and society.

In Part II, we examine the elements that are key to a law firm's sustainability strategy, including:

- the firm's culture, guided by a purpose;
- its clients, practices and sector focus;
- its people and talent, who should be aligned with its culture and be true experts who understand the ESG needs of clients;
- governance, risk management and compliance, including

management boards, risk evaluation and decision-making processes that govern the firm's development;
- its operations, including the associated carbon emissions; and
- its supply chain.

All these elements can contribute to a strategy that is comprehensively sustainable and puts society at the centre of everything the firm does.

Bringing benefits both to law firms and to society is both the objective of this Special Report and a product of sustainability. Profits for partners remain paramount for law firms. Otherwise, law firms will not be viable and will be unable to provide any positive impact in the longer run. This Special Report seeks not to denigrate profitable business, but rather to promote reflection on a new way of operating profitably that provides benefits to partners as well as to society. It aims to help partners think of new ways to conduct their business and to keep in sight the benefits (and negative effects) that their business can have on other stakeholders.

To ensure that these aspects are considered, law firms should begin by reflecting on their broader impact on the wider community and defining their purpose.

2. The underestimated power of culture and purpose

"*Culture eats strategy for breakfast.*"[36]

No strategy can be developed without first understanding how the firm operates, both officially and unofficially – whether because of its history, the habits of its people or its accepted non-documented processes.

There are four specific social sustainability dimensions of corporate culture which are predictors of financial success:

- sustainable strategy and leadership;
- mission communications and learning;
- social care and work life; and
- loyalty and identification.

There is a strong correlation between these four elements and the financial success of a firm.[37]

Culture, and the advantages of having a sincere and collectively developed purpose to embed that culture in everything the firm does, are the key pillars on which to develop a sustainable ESG strategy.

Figure 10. The business case for sustainability[38]

Firms that have a culture of sustainability are more successful financially

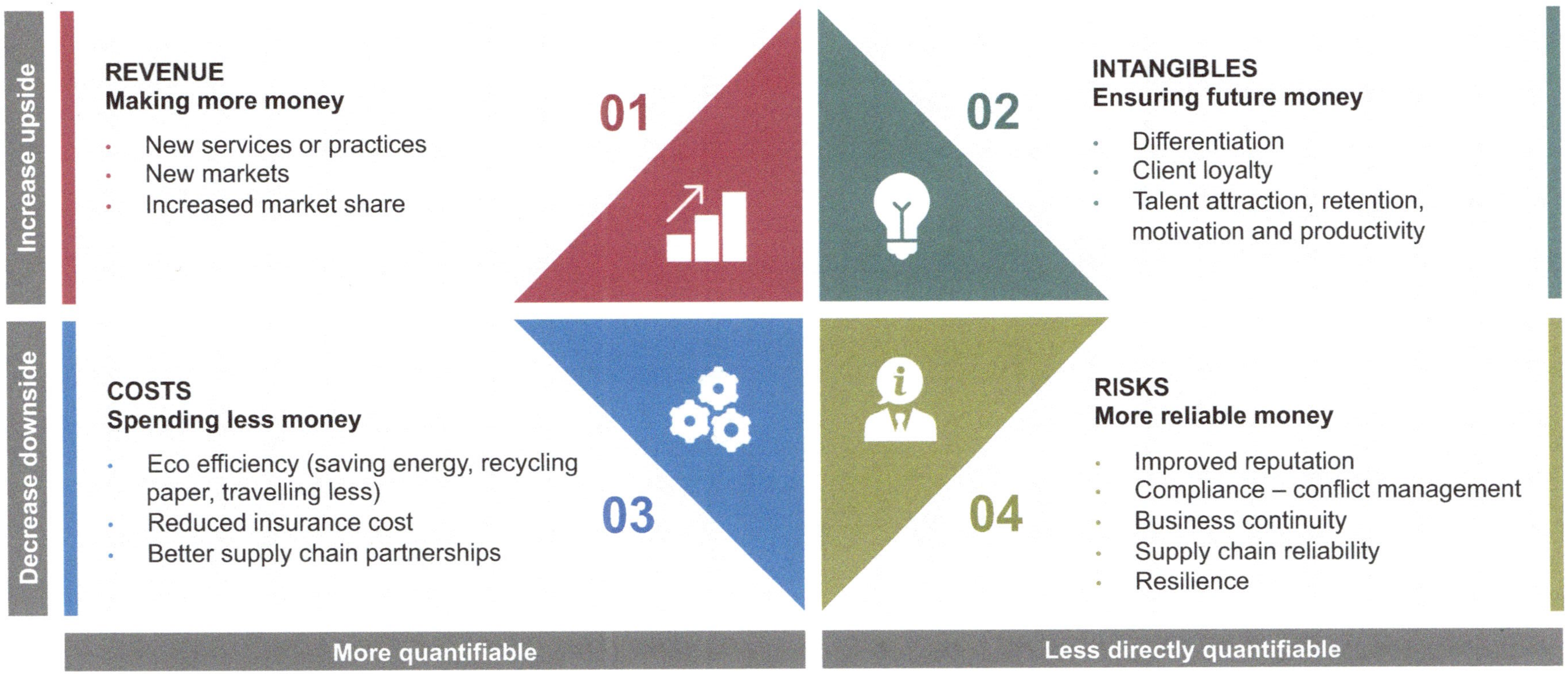

Source: Adapted from Andrew Winston, "The Business Case for Sustainability" (see n 38).

2.1 What is 'purpose'?

In this Special Report, we are not talking about purpose as the object of a law firm, but are rather referring to purpose in a wider sense.

Purpose is meaning; it is the cause for which a law firm exists. It responds to the question *why?* While it is easy to describe what a firm does and how it conducts its activities, it is often harder to articulate why it is useful, beyond the immediate financial reward it yields for its partners; and to whom it is useful, beyond immediate stakeholders and within society at large.

The purpose of a firm is expressed in a few chosen words that explain its reasons for existence and its long-term commitment to external constituents, and that define its 'licence to operate'. It is a guide or a compass that partners can call upon when determining the main objectives of their strategy, or that any member of the firm can refer to when deciding whether to take a particular action.

Purpose is not a CSR strategy. You can have one and not the other. A purpose describes the overarching objective that helps to define a firm's strategy, including its CSR strategy. A powerful starting point (although not the only starting point) for a firm that wants to define a sustainability strategy is to agree on a purpose.

2.2 Why a purpose?

Few law firms have formulated and adopted a real and meaningful purpose. Objections against formulating and committing to a purpose might include the following:

- Lawyers have a specific mission *per se* (ie, every client has the right to a lawyer);
- Lawyers are professionals in partnerships, rather than business corporations; and
- Lawyers do not need to seduce investors as they do not seek financing and cannot (in most jurisdictions) raise capital.

Some partners may also struggle to understand how a broad purpose can be useful for their business. Finally, in making a promise to the world, one cannot ignore the risks associated with a potential failure to comply with it.

But as more corporates embrace and communicate their purpose, the law firms that advise those corporates are acknowledging the need for a purpose of their own: both to 'walk the talk' and show their clients that they understand what they are talking about; and to demonstrate that they are modern business players that appreciate the competitive advantage a purpose can offer when sincere and truly implemented.

"The purpose of a firm is expressed in a few chosen words that explain its reasons for existence and its long-term commitment to external constituents, and that define its 'licence to operate'."

Law firms that have defined their purpose often give similar reasons for this move. Whether they are international business law firms based in different jurisdictions with different cultures or national firms undertaking different activities in different cities, larger firms need to define what makes them come together and identify the overarching principles that unite them. Developments in the legal sector that have fostered growing competition, market maturity and market segmentation are increasingly leading to a need for a purpose and core principles that act as guidelines for doing business and managing the firm.

2.3 The virtuous effects of purpose

The purpose of a firm can be extremely virtuous if the process of defining it is inclusive, comprehensive, transparent and honest. Developing a purpose should involve the partners and the firm at large, as well as all constituents of the firm, such as clients, suppliers and other entities with which the firm collaborates.

(a) Internally

Purpose provides motivation. People and talent appreciate that they are part of a bigger project and feel inspired by the broader goal.

Purpose also gives orientation. Firms with a purpose are more resilient and can find new ways to operate in unusual circumstances. Research has shown that defining a purpose becomes a key business priority in times of crisis. For example, during the COVID-19 pandemic, employees were more at ease in switching to remote working and continuing their activities autonomously when they were guided by the general principles provided by a purpose.[39]

Purpose is the glue that holds people together and develops a sense of belonging to the firm.

The younger generations are particularly keen on working for firms that have a genuine purpose; this can thus be a real asset in attracting and retaining talent. However, it is not about employer branding, but rather about ensuring there is a cultural fit and an alignment of objectives among all people in the organisation.

(b) Externally

To the outside world, a firm's purpose is an indication of what it stands for. It is a public undertaking that the firm will live up to its purpose and, conversely, a self-imposed obligation to respond to stakeholders such as NGOs, governments and other stakeholders.

A firm that communicates its purpose (which it should, as this sends out a clear message to constituents) should also expect to receive responses. This feedback should be actively sought out and collected. It can serve as a sounding board as to how the firm is doing and identify any gaps between the purpose statement and the way the firm's activities are perceived. It is a source for continuous improvement.

(c) Conduct of business and decision making

Establishing a purpose is not a one-off exercise. It involves engaging constituents in the process of establishing the purpose and then maintaining momentum while the purpose is formulated and communicated. Going forward, further effort is needed to keep the purpose alive while conducting business over time.

Day-to-day decisions will involve a balancing exercise. Resolving tensions and finding the right balance between more profit-driven decisions and more purpose-driven decisions will be a constant challenge.

2.4 Focus on recent regulation and case study in France

The French PACTE Law[40] – an action plan for business growth and transformation – enshrines the principle of corporate responsibility, stating in the Civil Code that "every commercial company must take account of the social and environmental impact of its activities".

Companies that want to take this to the next level may opt to include a purpose in their bylaws. In other words, in addition to describing what they do, corporates may choose to articulate why they do it, thus making a stronger commitment both to their employees and to the world at large.

Centaure was the first French law firm to establish a statutory purpose under the PACTE Law. Its statutory purpose reads as follows: "A company of legal intelligence, innovative, human and civic-minded, which responds to the rapidly changing needs of its clients by taking into account the societal and environmental impact of its development."[41] Each word in the purpose means something and is the fruit of extensive discussions between stakeholders. This process was inclusive and took place over nine months, as explained in Case Study 1.

Case Study 1

Living up to our statutory purpose

Laëtitia Cano, CSR and sustainable growth director, Centaure Avocats

> *The French PACTE Law gives companies the opportunity to include their purpose ('raison d'être') in their statutes. The partners of Centaure – a 35-lawyer firm operating in four different jurisdictions in France – decided to take this up. "It was a way of officially committing ourselves and providing us with a compass for the firm's strategy and governance; and of responding to the need for meaning that the members of the firm are looking for," explains Laëtitia Cano.*

Promoting engagement and unity: The commitment of the founding partner and the partners was strong. But we wanted to involve the whole firm through a sincere and inclusive approach. For our 20th anniversary, we wanted to bring together all members of the firm operating in our four locations by defining together what unites us.

Overcoming resistance to change: Yes, we have encountered resistance along the way! This is inherent in any process of change – especially when the model that has been in place for 20 years seems effective. Some people thought this was a passing fad and saw it merely as a desire to follow a new fashion, rather than a long-term evolution.

But in the end, it has helped us in structuring our choices. We thought about how to convince people; how to communicate effectively. Employees like to know and understand what is going on, beyond words – especially if their missions are affected by the transformation. It is therefore essential to involve them to secure their support. The process involved the members of our firm, clients, suppliers and colleagues, and took place over nine months.

Deciding on meaningful content: Finally, every word of our *raison d'être* is rich in meaning: "A firm of legal, human and civic intelligences that responds to the needs of its clients by caring about the societal and environmental impact of its development."

Our law firm sees itself as a 'company', a collective. Our clients are not those of the individual lawyers, but of the firm. Lawyers focus on their expertise and apply their legal intelligence to meet the rapidly changing needs of clients; while management functions are entrusted to specialist professionals.

Developing the *raison d'être* to bring it to life on a day-to-day basis over the long term: Discussions both within the firm and with our clients have enabled us not only to formalise our *raison d'être*, but also to define the five axes of its implementation. These axes inspire our daily actions in everything we do. Here are a few examples taken from our action plan, with concrete objectives:

- **Investment in people:** We have absorbed our Saint Ouen subsidiary into the group to develop an inter-bar structure. Our attachment to the Seine Saint Denis department (a less privileged area close to Paris) is also reflected in our partnerships with the universities of Paris XIII and Paris VIII to contribute to the training of the best students in the area. We regularly recruit our trainees and lawyers from this department.

  We also want to make progress on gender diversity in the partnership by building a pool of directors – the last step to partnership. The partner nominations this year have brought us from 18% to 30% of women partners.
- **Responsible purchasing:** We have rethought the living spaces of our firm. Our offices are places of work, but also of exchange, culture and sharing among professionals; places more adapted to our new way of working, closer to our clients, and including open spaces for working together and convivial spaces for interaction. We brought all the furniture from our old offices with us and upcycled it to adapt it to the new premises.
- **Digital ecology:** We have reduced our printing by 80% thanks to the digitalisation of our internal procedures and our communications with the courts. We have also put an end to mailing lists (we had 300 mailing lists in 2019) which clog up

mailboxes with useless 'reply to alls'. 'Copy to' must also be justified. It is forbidden to reply to an email with the original attachments. We still have a long way to go in terms of our digital ecology, but we are making progress!

- **Societal engagement:** Like many firms, we provide concrete help to the community (eg, donations of shoes and overalls to the care assistants of ADEF Residences; donations of computers to child welfare). But our civic commitment goes beyond donations and *pro bono* actions: we have integrated it into the heart of our activities, notably through our presence in the Saint Ouen area.
- **The development of a working ecosystem:** We choose our partners (eg, bailiffs, postulants, lawyers, service providers) with the same care as our employees, giving preference to those who share our values. We have been working with some of them for more than 20 years and they are moving in the same direction as us.

What's next? Our first objective is to consolidate and progress with what already exists and continue pursuing our five development axes in the coming years. This is a daily task. To further realise our ambitions, we will begin reporting on non-financial performance; will be assessed according to the ISO 26000 standard in 2022; and will participate in working groups in our sector to help other firms invest in a CSR policy. We also want to help our partners and clients to adopt this approach and to attract the younger generation who, above all, want to give meaning to their work.

3. The pivotal responsibility of law firms as advisers to their clients

"Taking responsibility is changing the core of your activities."[42]

A law firm can take ESG actions at various levels – for example, at the organisational level (eg, by embracing sustainable employment (see Part II, section 4) or by implementing a '3 Rs' policy (see Part II, section 6)). However, developing a sustainability strategy that also includes clients and practice groups will potentially have the biggest positive impact.

ESG is at the top of the agendas of general counsel. The increase in both the number and complexity of new regulations in general, and ESG regulations more specifically, and their significance for business keeps them awake at night.

Corporates are increasingly under pressure from employees, consumers, investors, activists and the media. General counsel –

"Lawyers can act as a bridge between the regulators and their clients, helping them to preserve their licence to operate by anticipating sustainability trends, even beyond existing regulations."

as the heads of legal, regulatory and compliance – are at the centre of this storm. ESG is a powerful and essential differentiator for law firms that can listen to and truly understand the rapid evolution of developments in this space, in order to provide the right services to assist clients with their transformation.

More than ever, ESG underlines the various capacities of a law firm. As a legal service provider, a law firm is both a legal adviser to its clients and a business partner with an in-depth understanding of the complex sectoral issues around sustainability. Lawyers can act as a bridge between the regulators and their clients, helping them to preserve their licence to operate by anticipating sustainability trends, even beyond existing regulations. Law firms are also independent economic actors in their own right and part of their clients' supply chains.

Clients require operational and strategic actions from their law firms at all levels. They expect their law firms to be role models and forward-looking advisers, as expressed by Martin Fischer in Case Study 2.

Case Study 2

The client perspective: the ESG transformation and its impact on law firms

Martin Fischer, board member, Fellowships at Auschwitz for the Study of Professional Ethics

ESG is top of the agenda for general counsel, who need comprehensive ESG services from law firms – and not only in terms of compliance. They are also looking to law firms for forward-looking integrity advice, and to serve as role models.

The ESG transformation

While interest in ESG issues has grown rapidly over the past five to 10 years, the COVID-19 pandemic has accelerated the trends relevant to ESG, such as decarbonisation, digitalisation, automation and e-commerce.

ESG has now become a crucial focus not only for governments, regulatory agencies and society, but also for companies and their employees, shareholders and customers. The issue of sustainability has thus reached a tipping point, with strong external and internal drivers pushing companies to do significantly more in terms of their ESG activities.

From a company perspective, the most influential external forces are:

- the numerous new laws and regulations being enacted, such as the European Green Deal and the German Supply Chain Due Diligence Act;
- customer expectations that companies will offer sustainable and low-carbon solutions;
- the courts as new stakeholders in this area (eg, the recent climate verdict of the German Federal Constitutional Court[i] and the *Shell* judgment of the Hague District Court in the Netherlands);[ii] and
- social and public pressure from very active NGOs and on social media.

i On 24 March 2021, the Federal Constitutional Court ruled that the provisions of the Climate Change Act of 12 December 2019 are incompatible with fundamental rights insofar as they lack sufficient requirements for further emission reductions from 2031 onwards.

ii On 26 May 2021, the Hague District Court ruled that Royal Dutch Shell must reduce carbon dioxide emissions from group activities by net 45% by the end of 2030, relative to 2019 levels.

One critical internal driver is employee engagement, as a company's ESG strategy is a decisive factor in attracting talent. This is reflected in the current 'purpose-driven' trend. Financial investors are another driver: they are increasingly adopting sustainable investment strategies as, like BlackRock, they now identify "climate risk as investment risk".

These fundamental transformations in the areas of economy, society, politics and technology can also be seen as the juridification of sustainability.

Shift from a 'compliance culture' to an 'integrity culture'

Given the proliferation of new ESG regulatory initiatives, in-house legal departments must play a critical role – not only by mitigating the potential risks, but also by creating strategic opportunities and facilitating ESG initiatives.

The requirements for responsible and entrepreneurial conduct in the sense of 'good corporate citizenship' have thus significantly increased. Internal legal advice is no longer limited to the pure legal consequences of business activities, but must also include a consideration of reputational risks, communication strategies and the expectations of financial investors and societal groups. This development can be described as a shift from a 'compliance culture' to an 'integrity culture'. Compliance work is thus evolving from the traditional focus on preventing corruption to encompass business advice on potential future issues.

Law firms as role models?

This seismic transformation of companies and change in the scope of in-house law departments will be directly reflected in how law firms deal with their clients.

One of the obvious impacts for law firms is the emergence of new areas of legal practice as a result of this trend, which will require them to become fully integrated ESG legal service providers. These include areas such as climate change, carbon trading, human rights, sustainable finance, environmental liabilities, ESG capital markets and CSR. Another component of this 'network advising' approach is the field of government relations, in order to manage legal risks arising from the political decision-making process.

Clients no longer expect their law firms to advise purely on legal risks and the legality of their actions. On the contrary, the focus should now be on the ethical dimensions of their advice. This means, in particular, considering the impact of ESG on business success. In addition, companies are already requiring their law firms to meet diversity criteria for project and advisory teams, and to mitigate their carbon footprints (eg, by changing their travel behaviour).

Meanwhile, laws firms must also meet the changing expectations of their own lawyers – especially in terms of applying ESG-related criteria internally and how they select their clients. ESG has further become a magnet for talent recruitment and retention.

The sole criterion of success for companies is swiftly moving away from increased profits or share prices towards positive impacts not only economically, but also socially and environmentally.

These new developments will expose law firms to potential dilemmas and challenges, as their own ESG values could conflict with the businesses and behaviour of their clients. How can a law firm promote ESG as an important factor and value in its business and financial decision making while defending the unsustainable businesses of its clients?

Individual lawyers, as responsible professionals at work and in the community, will need to ensure more than nominal compliance with established rules and to act with a significant new social responsibility. Therefore, law firms can and should act as role models for their clients, in terms of living ESG values both internally and externally.

3.1 The law firm as a legal adviser

In the capacity of legal advisers to their clients, law firms have a paramount role to play. As legal advisers, they can help their clients to understand:

- the ESG regulations that have been adopted in recent years and those which may be coming down the pipeline; and
- the implications that such regulations can have on clients' activities and business models.

These issues increasingly require lawyers to have a sophisticated business understanding, as well as sound and in-depth strategic legal knowledge of ESG.

(a) Structuring the offer/practice

In the recent past, practice groups focused on environmental law, territorial administrative law and human rights have been established both in full-service firms and in dedicated niche firms. Due to rapid advances in the issues around ESG and sustainability, many firms have renamed and strengthened their regulatory or environmental practice group as, for example, 'Environment and climate change'.

However, as ESG has now become a fundamental element of almost every aspect of (legal) business, each practice group is affected by ESG – not just the environmental practice group. As a result, practice groups must not only adapt to new ESG regulations, but also understand that a change in one area may have an impact on other practice areas and the activities of their clients. For example, if a manufacturing company cannot use a component of a product that is prohibited under new regulations, this may have implications that require it to review the composition of its entire product, its supply chain, its profitability and other issues, potentially giving rise to other legal challenges in different areas and even leading to a change in its business model.

So whatever the specific ESG needs of a client, the relevant practice groups must be able to navigate the labyrinth of new regulations. All practice groups encounter ESG issues, as illustrated in Figure 11 opposite; but most issues also involve other practice groups, which means that a cross-practice ESG team is needed to ensure a comprehensive and efficient view of all issues.

If law firms wish to continue advising their clients at a strategic level, they should develop an in-depth understanding of the full impact of ESG regulations on their clients and their clients' business models. The ESG implications will be very different depending on the client's respective business issues. Some clients are increasingly in need of proactive, forward-looking strategic advice. As a consequence, ESG-related issues require lawyers to have an in-depth understanding of trends and developments in ESG regulation, as well as the challenges, threats and opportunities for clients, and the implications for their sectors and industries. Lawyers are increasingly expected to provide comprehensive, holistic and forward-looking counsel on ESG-related matters.

This is why many firms are now structuring their ESG services in a cross-practice ESG offering, enabling them to provide more comprehensive advice. Internally, lawyers are learning to work across different practice groups and understand ESG issues more comprehensively. They can thus provide a more informed, more seamless service, as well as being more efficient and guiding clients from one practice area across other areas of the firm.

As an illustration, Gide has created Gide Impact – a virtual practice that sits across traditional service lines and that can respond to virtually any client's needs with respect to its sustainability transformation. Didier G Martin explains how Gide Impact was developed in Case Study 3 on page 50.

Figure 11. Integrated ESG practice

Firms with an integrated ESG practice can create more value for clients in multiple areas

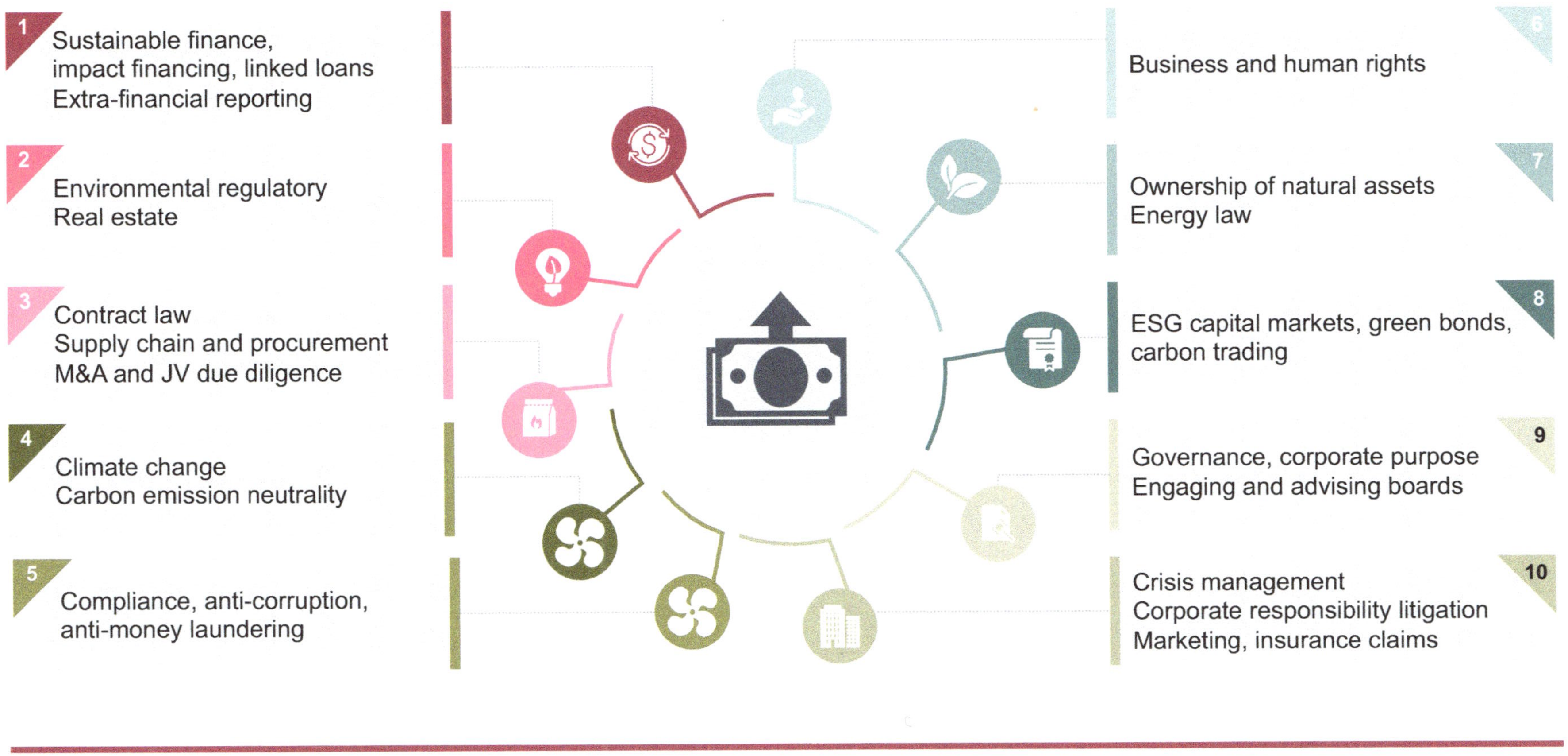

Source: Venturis Consulting Group, all rights reserved.

Case Study 3

Developing a multi-disciplinary ESG practice

Didier G Martin, M&A partner, coordinator of the ESG practice and co-chair of the Sustainable Development Commission, Gide Loyrette Nouel; and **Eleanor Forshaw**, *pro bono* coordinator, Gide Loyrette Nouel

Over the past few years, Gide Loyrette Nouel – an international law firm of French origin founded in 1920, with 500 lawyers in 10 offices worldwide – has moved from improving its own CSR to helping clients take better account of all ESG-related legal matters.

Gide's first concrete action in terms of CSR related to *pro bono* work. Gide was one of the first firms in France to formalise this through a proper policy, back in 2011. The policy allows all members of the firm to spend up to 40 hours of their working time on *pro bono* matters approved by the firm's dedicated *pro bono* commission and count these hours towards annual worktime objectives. This *pro bono* work is coupled with an endowment fund, which receives €250,000 per year from all partners of the firm.

Gide has since increased its actions with respect to CSR, publishing a dedicated report every two years since 2014 covering *pro bono*, HR and environmental matters. Diversity workgroups and a sustainable development commission, involving partners, associates and employees, have been created to spearhead the firm's CSR policies. Together with *pro bono*, these are the three key aspects of the firm's CSR commitment.

While there is still work to do on all these issues, the firm decided some time ago that, as well as striving to improve its own CSR, it could also help clients to improve theirs.

Over the past 10 years, Gide identified the need to increase its practice in the fields of environmental law and compliance, and proceeded with lateral hires to strengthen its teams specialising on these topics. As a full-service firm, Gide also realised that in various practice areas, such as finance and compliance, clients were becoming increasingly sensitive to ESG issues. In 2018, lawyers of the firm supported a move in favour of the legal recognition of companies with extended business purpose, or mission-led companies ('*sociétés à mission*').

In 2019, a group of Gide lawyers with a particular interest in ESG matters established a multi-disciplinary team, Gide Impact, to assist clients with all legal matters relating to the risks and opportunities of ESG. This step was quite innovative at the time in France. The team's role was primarily to identify the various fields of law that were impacted by the growing importance of ESG and involve motivated lawyers within the firm who were addressing or wished to address these issues, to deepen their expertise and knowledge and share ideas and promote initiatives with a view to offering appropriate advice to clients – be they companies or financial players – to assist them with all legal aspects of ESG.

Gide Impact now comprises partners from various practices of the firm – including M&A, corporate, litigation, compliance, finance, employment, environment and economic law – who are members of associations or thinktanks involved in ESG, or speakers at conferences or webinars on related topics. The team has officially become a full practice group of the firm, called "CSR, ESG, sustainability (Gide Impact)".

Gide now regularly assists clients on matters such as:

- French due diligence law, according to which French corporations must identify and mitigate risks to human rights, health and the environment in their supply chains;
- litigation related to climate or human rights;
- the establishment of shareholders' foundations;
- the process of becoming mission-led companies ('*sociétés à mission*');
- non-financial reporting obligations;
- ESG-related activism;
- the creation of impact funds; and
- the issuance of green bonds.

In the past few years, Gide has thus moved from improving its own CSR to increasingly helping clients to take better account of all ESG-related legal matters, at a time when hard law is covering an ever-growing number of ESG matters and when the risk of litigation brought by stakeholders is also increasing significantly.

(b) Innovation catalyst

ESG can also be an innovation catalyst for law firms – and their practice and sector groups – to develop ESG-compliant services and products. For example:

- banking and financing practices must increasingly consider ESG-related terms and conditions, such as:
  - results-oriented loans, with interest rates linked to environmental improvement; and

  - social linked bonds, with interest rates linked to the positive social impact created (eg, the number of jobs created or the number of people having access to finance);
- corporate/M&A practices will need to add ESG-related issues to their due diligence processes – not only from a legal perspective, but also from a reputational perspective; and
- dispute resolution practices will need to adapt to a relatively new reality in which corporate and even governmental clients are sued by NGOs in order to force them to commit to and/or comply with (non-)legal binding pledges they have made (or not made).

One may question whether some of these developments are true examples of innovation; but the fact is that law firms, and their respective practice and sector groups, have abundant opportunities and challenges to develop new services and deliver added value in relation to their existing legal services. Irrespective of the type of practice, ESG will have an impact on advice and transactions that goes beyond the legal perspective. For example, reputation and communication will become issues that lawyers cannot ignore. While some law firms are expanding their offers internally, others are establishing partnerships with other consultancy specialists (eg, in crisis communications) to offer top-quality, highly skilled packaged services.

(c) Opening up new markets

ESG innovation also opens up new markets for lawyers. Technology is a significant enabler in this field. For example, a law firm that specialises in contract negotiation may develop (or partner with a legal tech firm to develop) a document generation and automation tech product which can be used to help lawyers prepare standard documents for clients in a faster, more efficient way. It could also be used to provide people in developing countries in need of basic legal documentation with a standard, reliable and fast service at a decent cost. Law firms can reach more clients with an adapted service at a lower margin, bringing benefits both to the firm and to society, and contributing towards the achievement of SDG 16.

The vast ESG space now allows lawyers to play a distinctive and proactive role in designing legal tools to facilitate positive impact.

ESG is becoming part of the legal community

Dedicated legal practices such as environmental law (including climate change), business and human rights, and corporate investigations and anti-corruption have existed for some time. To a certain extent, these disciplines form the basis of what we now call 'ESG law'. However, the fact that ESG law is now considered an overarching legal practice confirms that this discipline has truly come of age.

Rankings and awards in the international legal sector are flourishing. Various law firms have received acclaim as the best places to work for women, for innovation or for their human rights or *pro bono* efforts. Until recently, ESG issues were ranked within their respective practice areas; but ESG has now become a new cross-practice topic. Legal directory *Chambers and Partners* recently introduced an ESG risk management ranking for law firms; *The Legal 500* is launching its *Global Green Guide*; and the *Financial Times* now rewards ESG actions and awarded the FT Innovative Lawyers 2021 Award to Hausfeld for its global climate litigation work on behalf of Greta Thunberg and its petition filed with the UN Committee on the Rights of the Child.

The significance of ESG is also highlighted daily on social media and in newspapers, documentaries and the legal press. As such, it has become an important marketing tool for law firms. Rankings and awards are great business development, marketing and communication tools; but with ESG, this could easily backfire into greenwashing or social washing.

See *Chambers and Partners*' Global Environmental, Social & Governance Risk Legal Rankings at https://chambers.com/legal-rankings/enironmental-social-governance-risk-law-firms-global-wide-96:3141:15649:1 and *The Legal 500 Global Green Guide* at www.legal500.com/global-green-guide/.

3.2 The law firm as business adviser with sector knowledge

Sustainability has become an overarching challenge and opportunity for all organisations; it will set the new standards for doing business. However, not every corporate, sector or industry is equally affected by ESG. Due to their specific business models, certain sectors and industries have a greater negative impact on, for example, the environment or human and workers' rights. As a consequence, the types of assistance and capabilities that clients require from law firms will vary depending on their business, sector and industry.

Clients' transition to increased responsibility and sustainability:

- requires substantial and systemic changes to their respective business models, including supply chains; and
- presents law firms with interesting opportunities and challenges to assist them with this transition and to work together with and advise all relevant stakeholders.

"Law firms are also increasingly coming under pressure for their own activity in certain sectors – for example, from activist groups such as Extinction Rebellion, which have protested against law firms' ties to the oil and gas industry."

It is clear that law firms must evolve to become true business partners of their clients, with in-depth knowledge and understanding of the full impact of ESG at sector and industry level. Law firms are also increasingly coming under pressure for their own activity in certain sectors – for example, from activist groups such as Extinction Rebellion, which have protested against law firms' ties to the oil and gas industry.[43]

The Meadows Report highlighted oil as a potentially finite resource whose continued exploitation at current levels is unsustainable in the long run. Major oil pollution incidents have also put the industry in the spotlight. Young workers also criticise oil companies as being ecologically unfriendly and therefore do not consider them good places to work. At the same time, however, the sector is key in providing access to energy to all and – with its vast financial resources, capabilities and know-how – will play a crucial role in the transition to clean and sustainable energy.[44]

Another (potential) ESG headache for law firms is the fashion industry. This is one of the largest industries in the world: with $3 trillion in turnover, it accounts for 2% of global gross domestic product and employs 430 million people.[45] After the oil and gas sector, it is the second most polluting industry worldwide. The use of chemicals in textile treatment and the excessive use of water cause severe damage to the environment; while serious accidents in textile factories in developing countries are a common occurrence[46] and workers are frequently exploited. However, the fashion industry is gradually moving towards more responsible and sustainable supply chains.[47]

In this complex environment, law firms must strike a balance between:

- their own business and financial interests;
- their reputations;
- the needs that their clients satisfy;
- the key roles that many of their clients are playing in the transition to sustainability; and
- (especially for lawyers, a convincing argument) the fact that certain irresponsible, unsustainable and/or polluting activities of their clients still constitute legitimate business.

Those firms that have engaged in a sector approach – that is, which have developed a thorough understanding of the challenges in specific sectors and which share best practices across the firm – will be better equipped than their rivals.

3.3 The law firm as a bridge between regulators, society and business

Next comes the difficult discussion about the wider role of law firms to inspire and lead. Beyond stating the law as it currently stands and anticipating future regulations that are under discussion, should law firms develop a more comprehensive understanding of the major issues worldwide and play an active role in helping governments to draft regulations to address them, or suggest that their clients do more beyond pure compliance?

What role should lawyers play in influencing the regulators to adopt or adapt rules? At first sight, as lawyers represent the interests of their clients, it is questionable whether their lobbying would serve a wider social and environmental purpose. But what if lawyers took a broader perspective, aimed at reconciling the interests of their clients with those of society? In the sustainability arena, either we all win or we all lose. Lawyers stand at the crossroads of the transition to a sustainable world, helping regulators to enact ESG laws[48] and helping clients to play a sustainable role, even beyond existing regulations.

In this Special Report, we demonstrate the business case for sustainability and highlight the pivotal role that lawyers should play in developing this business case, both for themselves and for their clients. The role of lawyers is to:

- raise awareness among clients of the necessary and inevitable role that businesses have in contributing to the SDGs;
- adopt new ways of (sustainable) thinking and altered business mores (ie, what is legally justified is not necessarily strategically desirable), and promote these to clients; and
- make sustainability at minimum an essential criterion for their licence to operate and, even further, a source of competitive advantage both for their clients and for themselves.

The lawyer of the future will serve as a bridge between society, policymakers and regulators and businesses, understanding the positions and arguments of all sides and finding solutions in the common interests of all. Acting an 'influencer' in the noble sense of the term, the lawyer of the future will have to be diplomatic and truly willing to reach out to all stakeholders and other parties. Pure activists will not succeed; neither will excellent lawyers with high-quality drafting skills. The lawyer of the future will develop a true competitive advantage by reflecting the big picture in their advice, including the SDGs.

3.4 The law firm as independent economic actor and part of client supply chains

Lawyers are not just legal advisers; they must also have an in-depth understanding of the trends and developments in clients' businesses and sectors, as well as of ESG-related issues. But more so, clients will have certain expectations of a firm's own activities as a business.

Clients have significant responsibilities in terms of their legal and tax obligations, ESG commitments and reputations. Moreover, they are increasingly being held responsible for their actions by society, stakeholders and NGOs. In this respect, clients must not only take the necessary steps themselves, but also ensure that all players in their global supply chains – including their legal service providers – are compliant with their own cultures, values and positions on ESG issues.

These developments are reflected in the process through which clients appoint their law firms. Clients increasingly request firms to show their commitment to ESG issues from the initial request for proposal and pitch phase. These requirements – which many firms may previously have regarded as a mere 'tick-the-box' exercise – are taken increasingly seriously, both by law firms and by their clients. Topics such as D&I, net zero, risk management, human rights and anti-corruption processes now feature in many requests for proposals. It is now more common for a firm to lose a pitch due to a lack of team diversity or a lack of sincerity in the reporting of ESG practices. Moreover, clients are exerting pressure on law firms to engage in their ESG journey: for example, one multinational withholds part of the remuneration due to its law firms if D&I targets are not met. As with many trends and developments in the international legal sector, clients have been the main driver of change with regard to ESG within law firms.

4. The law firm as a sustainable employer

Clients have justified expectations of their legal service providers in terms of ESG; but so too do employees and associates, whose expectations have a significant impact on talent management. More than ever, and as in many sectors and industries, young lawyers are no longer just looking for a job; they are looking for a meaningful job. A job where they are listened to; where they can contribute to the organisation and the management; where they can have (as an integral part of their professional activities) a positive impact on their communities; and where they can have a decent work-life balance.

Talent expectations are discussed by Franziska Adelmann in Case Study 4.

Case Study 4

Why we should expect more responsibility from law firms
Franziska Adelmann, law student, Bucerius Law School

Talent are increasingly keen to join firms with a well-thought-out CSR strategy, as expressed in this young professional's thoughts on CSR in the legal profession.

One of the most important reasons why I decided to spend five years of my life studying law was the people. I was excited by the precise, well-structured way in which lawyers work, and by their dedication. Lawyers pride themselves on their problem-solving skills. This is exactly why law firms should put their collective intelligence and skills to good use and solve some of the world's problems – or at the very least, not make them worse.

"But how exactly should they do that?" you may ask. In my opinion, a great place to start is by developing a CSR strategy. This does not mean that you cannot have a positive impact without one; but it means that you can increase your impact in a more intentional way.

CSR has so many elements – from the firm's ecological footprint to its responsibility towards employees; from the firm's impact on the outside world through its choice of clients to the provision of *pro bono* legal services or voluntary work. While there are many great approaches to these individual elements, I am still looking for a law firm with a convincing strategy that covers all elements of CSR.

While green energy, reduced air travel and travel generally, diversity and mental health, as well as great *pro bono* projects, have all found their way into many major law firms, there seems to be some hesitancy concerning the selection criteria for clients and their transparent communication. You might argue that everyone has a right to legal representation, and that the main goal of a law firm is to earn money from its services. However, if you want your strategy to be taken seriously, it must be reflected in your choice of clients and the instructions you take on. Everyone has the right to legal representation, but that does not mean that everyone has the right to your specific legal representation.

Improvements in any aspect of CSR must be supported and driven by the management of the firm. However, it is just as important to get all employees on board. In my opinion, you can achieve this by encouraging your teams to choose a CSR topic to focus on and incentivising them to spend one day every six months on developing their strategy and evaluating their progress.

What matters most to me is transparency. Students can only form an opinion about which firm best fits their individual values based on honest communication about CSR. Personally, I will always respect a firm that mentions the areas in which it is still trying to improve more than a firm which just lists its successes. I want to be able to learn about a law firm's values and CSR strategy from its website or during interviews. If I talk to an intern who has been working for a firm for two weeks, I want them to be able to answer questions on the different elements of CSR – not because they had to watch a mandatory video, but because these are reflected in their daily work. It is also great if they know whom to approach when they have an idea for change.

If you believe that I am holding law firms to a very high standard, just imagine what kind of positive impact a small change to a law firm's strategy can have. Changing the approach and focus of the lawyers working in a firm has a multiplier effect on every personal and professional interaction.

Personally, I am excited about making the world a better place and using the skills I have acquired during my studies to do so. For my future to lead me to a law firm, we need to share the same goals.

Moreover, talent increasingly hold firms (as potential employers) responsible for their role in society. Examples of collective action include a student association which provides law firms with climate change scorecards[49] and student sit-ins against law firms representing certain clients.[50]

"Young lawyers do care about their remuneration; however, high remuneration alone will not prevent them from leaving their firm or the profession."

On top of these challenging developments, a recent global survey of young lawyers around the world conducted by the International Bar Association (IBA) and Acritas highlighted six main points of concern and suggested some actions from current management of law firms in response:[51]

- Young lawyers do care about their remuneration; however, high remuneration alone will not prevent them from leaving their firm or the profession.
- An important concern for their future in the profession is maintaining a sustainable work-life balance and general well-being.
- Young lawyers wish to understand technological developments and their applications in the legal world, and are keen to train in legal technology.
- Law firms should actively seek to improve their workplace cultures.
- Law firms should recover quickly from the COVID-19 pandemic and embed more flexible working and increased use of technology.
- Communication is key. Young lawyers want to be given the opportunity to speak up and suggest ideas. Firms must not only organise feedback sessions, but also report and take action based on the feedback received.

The talent management functions of law firms will need to develop strategies that both address the firm's varied roles[52] and reflect the fast-changing needs that ESG demands from law firms, with regard to both their clients and their people. Firms can preserve their licence to operate by responding reactively; or, by addressing these developments proactively, can even turn their talent strategies into a driver of competitive advantage.

Priorities for talent management will include:

- ensuring well-being and a good work-life balance;
- providing a meaningful job for lawyers;
- organising personal and career development in a sustainable way; and
- managing diversity.

4.1 Ensuring well-being and a good work-life balance

Burnout is all too common in the legal sector, as lawyers are pushed to their limits by the punishing working hours and non-sustainable working practices of traditional law firms. Firms must daily strike a balance between demanding client work, heavy workloads and financial targets on the one hand, and the long-term preservation of the health and well-being of their lawyers on the other. A recent

"Concerning and increasing levels of depression, stress, addiction and suicide are reported in the legal profession."

survey conducted for the *Financial Times Innovative Lawyers (Europe) Report*[53] revealed that despite the higher salaries on offer, an increasing number of lawyers do not wish to join or return to big law firms because of the workloads involved; and 90% of lawyers in search of a job regard well-being and mental health as key elements in choosing a job.

The issue of well-being is increasingly being recognised by law firms and is top of mind for their leadership:

- More law firms are monitoring working hours, both to ensure that everyone is busy enough and to intervene where individuals are exceeding reasonable working hours. For example, one law firm[54] has appointed a dedicated support person with responsibility for resource planning to monitor hours worked and another person with responsibility for holiday planning, to ensure that lawyers benefit from their minimum guaranteed holiday.
- Examples of concrete programmes that have long been successfully pursued by law firms to promote a balanced lifestyle include encouraging sports (eg, creating sports rooms in office buildings, providing subscriptions to sports clubs) and providing facilities and concierge services (eg, laundry, concierge, manicure, hairdresser or massage).
- An interesting example of collaborations between employers to tackle the issue is the Mindful Business Charter[55] – a collective effort to promote healthier and more effective ways of working in the legal sector which was launched by Addleshaw Goddard, Pinsent Mason and Barclays, and which has since been adopted by many other law firms. Similarly, Clifford Chance launched the Global Business Collaboration for Better Workplace Mental Health[56] together with leading cross-sector global businesses such as HSBC, Deloitte, Unilever, Salesforce and BHP.
- In October 2021 the IBA launched a major study across all continents and types of legal systems.[57] The findings revealed common elements across the board: concerning and increasing levels of depression, stress, addiction and suicide are reported in the legal profession. In addition, there is a stigma attached to depression and anxiety problems, and lawyers are reluctant to talk about them openly, assuming that they are unavoidable or even something to be proud of. While law firms recognise that this is an issue, very few of them are tackling the problem with clear action plans. The IBA recommends[58] that firms address this well-being crisis through four steps:
    - Adopt a well-being policy, prepared collaboratively throughout the firm;
    - Address systemic problems and their underlying causes (eg,

    lack of managerial training, harassment, bullying, sexism, racism and more generally a culture of unsustainable working hours);
  - Prioritise mental well-being, encourage people to discuss it and ensure that leadership act as role models, to allay fears of any repercussions for careers; and
  - Recognise difficulties experienced in particular by certain groups and strengthen efforts to foster equality of opportunities and inclusion in the workplace.
- More is now being done to promote sustainable behaviours. Examples include:
  - adopting a zero-tolerance policy to inappropriate behaviours;
  - developing anti-harassment rules; and
  - setting responsible and reasonable billable-hours targets, or getting rid of them altogether.
- Induced and accelerated by the COVID-19 crisis, firms must also develop policies on remote working, working from home, flexible offices and part-time work. These developments will involve a total change in working habits and methodologies will need to be carefully thought out.

4.2 Providing a meaningful job for lawyers

However, as outlined above, there is much more to being a sustainable employer than simply taking care of employees' mental well-being and ensuring a good work-life balance. If one thing has become clear over the past decade, it is that young talent are increasingly looking for meaningful jobs; they want to be part of the bigger picture and contribute to something inspiring. If they wish to keep their 'licence to operate', law firms have no choice but to provide talent with meaningful jobs. The innovative ways in which they do so may provide them with a competitive advantage.

In practice, a meaningful job could involve:

- contributing to the context and becoming involved in the firm's management or directions (see Part II, section 5);
- understanding client strategy and having a say in the types of clients and instructions accepted; or
- participating in *pro bono* initiatives.

(a) Selective work

The younger generations are truly concerned about current global challenges such as global warming, decreasing biodiversity, poverty and pollution. The tension between what they stand for as private individuals and what their firms expect from them professionally is no longer theoretical. Firms are increasingly confronted with questions and even (mild) resistance from everyone from junior associates to partners (and even law students) about the types of clients and instructions that they accept.

Law firms must ask themselves: "Do we want to defend that oil company in court against charges relating to the pollution it generates? Do we want to draft financing and loan agreements for clients active in the palm oil industry? Do we want to work for clients in the fashion industry that are still producing clothes in unsafe factories?"

Talent has become more selective about the types of clients, sectors and activities they wish to service. As a consequence, firms need to start thinking about what these developments mean for their talent management strategies and policies.

(b) Pro bono

The *pro bono* programmes that firms run – often as part of their CSR policy – can play a key role here. Most law firms have some kind of *pro bono* programme, which:

- responds to their roles and (perceived) responsibilities in society (ie, to increase their societal impact);
- facilitates the ambitions and aspirations of individual lawyers (ie, to do meaningful work); and
- serves as a marketing and communications tool.

"Young talent are increasingly looking for meaningful jobs; they want to be part of the bigger picture and contribute to something inspiring."

Pro bono programmes make a significant contribution towards the sustainability efforts of law firms. However, there are two specific challenges that firms must address to avoid falling into the trap of 'greenwashing' (or 'social washing').

Time spent on *pro bono* matters: The first trap relates to the financial structure of the firm and how it deals with resourcing and time spent on *pro bono* clients and matters. If a *pro bono* programme is seen as how the firm can contribute to the community and help lawyers realise their ambitions and aspirations, the financial performance structure must value the time spent on *pro bono* matters in the same way as time spent on firm clients and matters. The trap is that – despite policies that support this approach – individual partners still afford higher value to billable hours (ie, those spent on firm clients and their matters).

Tension between *pro bono* clients and firm clients: The second trap concerns the firm's reputation and credibility. Firms work for all types of clients, sectors and industries. For example, they may undertake significant legal work for a client operating in the cattle breeding industry;[59] and their legal work could (indirectly) contribute to clients' unsustainable activities.[60] On the other hand, firms handle *pro bono* matters because they want to make a positive contribution and assume greater responsibility – for instance, by assisting a start-up that aims to protect the seas and oceans. At this point, firms are increasingly confronted with concerns and questions both from the outside world and from their own groups of professionals about how their *pro bono* work aligns with their less sustainable practices.

There is still some way to go before this contradiction can be resolved. Is *pro bono* a firm commitment – one that attracts and retains talent and creates a competitive advantage? Or is it a mere 'tick-the-box' exercise that engages individual lawyers on a voluntary basis without affecting overall firm practices? Talent will quickly spot the difference.

4.3 Personal and career development in the age of sustainability

ESG, the SDGs, well-being, *pro bono* work, a meaningful job – all of these elements must become part of the personal and career development programmes of law firms. Lawyers look for opportunities for personal development when deciding whether to join – and stay at – a law firm. Training and development, particularly in relation to ESG, are clearly key motivations and retention factors (as well as a competitive advantage for clients).

(a) Training

The training curriculum is evolving as sustainability increases in importance. In addition to traditional training, more development programmes are conducted jointly with clients. Firms are entering into partnerships with clients involving training, secondments and *pro bono* initiatives.

As they recognise the increased client demand for ESG services, law firms must ensure that their lawyers receive the necessary training in ESG. As an example, Linklaters established an ESG Accelerator Programme to ensure that senior lawyers and partners develop the necessary understanding of sustainability theory, climate change and numerous regulatory developments. The training encompasses all other areas of the law which are impacted by these issues (eg, litigation, M&A, initial public offerings, finance, general corporate law).[61]

Most firms, realising that sustainability is top of mind for their clients, provide training, seminars, podcasts and webinars on sustainability to raise awareness and give their clients the tools to drive business in a sustainable manner.

Training and development around the SDGs are priorities for the business world. The whole topic of sustainability is new and evolving for everyone. All business actors are learning – both clients and lawyers. In one innovative initiative, upmarket French firm August Debouzy has launched a think tank which brings together clients and legal experts to exchange ideas and collaborate on necessary transformation journeys. This is an area where lawyers can leverage their role as advisers on business transitions.

(b) Career development

As law firms build out their career development functions, they are seeking to include sustainability in everything they offer to their talent (eg, formal and regular feedback processes, career paths, promotion milestones), to develop employees' potential both within and outside the firm. Although these efforts are not new, they are now being more widely shared among law firms.

Providing regular feedback – whether on the job during or immediately after an assignment or at regular formal checkpoints quarterly or annually – is a way of treating people fairly and helping them to grow and progress; and in itself is a sustainable way of conducting business.

(c) Evaluation processes

Over the past decade, a growing number of firms have adopted evaluation processes that take into account both financial and non-financial performance. Firms that have formulated a sustainability strategy should include ESG performance criteria which can be

"Firms that truly want to walk the talk and put sustainability at the centre of their strategies should design a promotion process that includes indicators showing the contribution that applicants have made towards achieving the firm's key strategic objectives."

measured against annual business planning; in other words, there cannot be a transparent performance review without a clear business planning process. As a consequence, firms that have developed a sustainability strategy should formulate criteria, objectives and activities that contribute to this strategy and can be evaluated in a clear and transparent way at a personal and practice group level.

(d) Promotion criteria

It is possible to make promotion contingent on the applicant's contribution to enhancing the firm's sustainability, whether through client work, firm management activities or *pro bono* services. Where two competent lawyers have worked equally hard, priority should be given to the lawyer who has had the greatest positive impact on the firm's communities. Worthy of special mention in this regard is Hogan Lovells, the first international firm to promote a full-time *pro bono* lawyer to partnership.[62]

Firms that truly want to walk the talk and put sustainability at the centre of their strategies should design a promotion process that includes indicators showing the contribution that applicants have made towards achieving the firm's key strategic objectives, including the SDGs.

4.4 Diversity, inclusion and equality of opportunities

D&I is considered as a specific issue in the ESG agenda.[63] Most law firms provide dedicated resources and budgets, appoint separate functions, design specific goals and present the topic as a separate section on their websites.

Clients have been the main driver for greater D&I in law firms. Even 10 years ago, it was common practice for a law firm to lose a pitch due to a lack of team diversity – mainly gender based at the time. We have recently seen a multinational withhold part of a law firm's remuneration if D&I targets are not met. Clients are thus finding ways to encourage – and even compel – law firms to progress on their diversity journey.

The scope of diversity is now understood more widely and includes gender balance, LGBTI+, ethnicity, disability, religion and age.

Most law firms are working to ensure equality of opportunities for members across the board, including in relation to:

- recruitment;
- career development;
- assignment of instructions;
- access to promotion;
- equal pay; and
- pay rises.

The difficulty is that proactive steps are needed to change the status quo, embedded in cultures, habits, biases and misperceptions.

(a) Gender balance

Beyond fairness and equity, which are often mentioned as reasons why law firms should pay particular attention to SDG 5 in their strategies, there are important business drivers for putting this issue at the top of their agendas.

Extensive research has demonstrated that mixed teams are more efficient and profitable. It is thus unsurprising that this is a key priority for most law firms.

Drivers of business performance: Law firms are increasingly making efforts to promote diversity at all levels of the organisation in order to improve their business performance[64] by:

- meeting client demands;
- inspiring innovation;
- ensuring regulatory compliance;

- attracting talent; and
- enhancing leadership effectiveness.

Clients: Clients' businesses have become more diverse; today, more general counsel are female than ever before. Women are key to legal services purchasing decisions and law firms must ensure that partners understand and take account of their clients' evolution in this regard. Partners will find it easier to act in partnership with their clients if they have been trained to notice gender biases, which too often are inadvertently ignored.

Innovation: General counsel, whether men or women, are looking for the most innovative advice. Innovation often results from a confluence of different viewpoints, backgrounds and experiences. This is why genuine diversity is a key criterion in law firms' selection processes.

Regulations: Equality of opportunities is a constitutional right in most Western jurisdictions. Law firms are now scrutinised on this issue as part of clients' supply chains. Discrimination is a compliance, reputational and financial risk.

Talent: In Western jurisdictions, the proportion of female lawyers is growing. In the United States, while about 47% of all associates are women, only 31% of non-equity partners and 21% of all equity partners are women.[65] In France, 57% of lawyers but 30% of equity partners are women.[66] Recent research from *The Lawyer* revealed that partner diversity in the top 50 City law firms is below 30%.[67] So are law firms attracting and retaining the world's best talent?

Leadership: To innovate and lead effectively in today's globalised multicultural environment, a law firm needs a diverse team at board level, which is representative of its workforce and clientele.

Representation in the profession: Law firms are proactively working to become more diverse and inclusive. Women are often well represented in associate recruitment. In France, for instance, 70% of law school graduates are women,[68] and similar trends can be observed in other Western countries.

In terms of equal pay, major law firms have established salary grids to ensure fair remuneration and prevent unconscious bias. However, although regulations, employee pressure, court rulings and growing care around these issues have resulted in improvements and reduced inequalities, the risk of discrimination remains a point of vigilance, in law firms as in every business.

More generally, women tend to leave the profession more frequently than men, after four or five years in the job and certainly before partner level.[69] The patterns look similar in a number of law firms (see Figure 12 overleaf). It is argued that this unwanted turnover of female lawyers translates into financial loss for law firms.

Five simultaneous workstreams to encourage gender diversity: To prevent this unwanted attrition and ensure that women remain and grow with them, law firms should work simultaneously on five workstreams which should be embedded in their core strategy.

Engage top management: Top management have an important role to play in engaging and explaining the importance of gender diversity throughout the firm. They must walk the talk and ensure parity, or accurate representativity, at board level (see Part II, section 5 on governance).

Change the culture: Changing the culture involves raising awareness of different behaviours and the benefits of gender diversity among all lawyers in a firm – male and female, associates and partners. It involves proactively developing practices to achieve a better work-life balance for all lawyers. These processes must be conducted collaboratively with men – in particular, to reassure mid-level male lawyers who may feel that they will be left behind.

Equip women: Some law firms develop talent pools at all levels, ensuring that a mix of candidates is involved in each recruitment or promotion round and widening the age brackets from which to promote to partnership. Firms must also support the development of women, provide training to increase their influence, organise mentorships and encourage networking.

Adapt the rules of the game: The processes in place for promotion and development can involve unconscious bias or be insufficiently inclusive.

Law firms should continually review their appraisal forms to ensure they include non-biased and objective performance criteria. For instance, references to subjective terms such as 'ambition' or 'resistance to stress' may be interpreted with unconscious bias.

The promotion process can easily be adapted so that final-stage interviews can only be arranged if at least one woman and one man are on the shortlist.

Law firms can also break the cycle of linear career development and reward different experience or promote some lawyers to partnership

Figure 12. Example of a seniority career chart

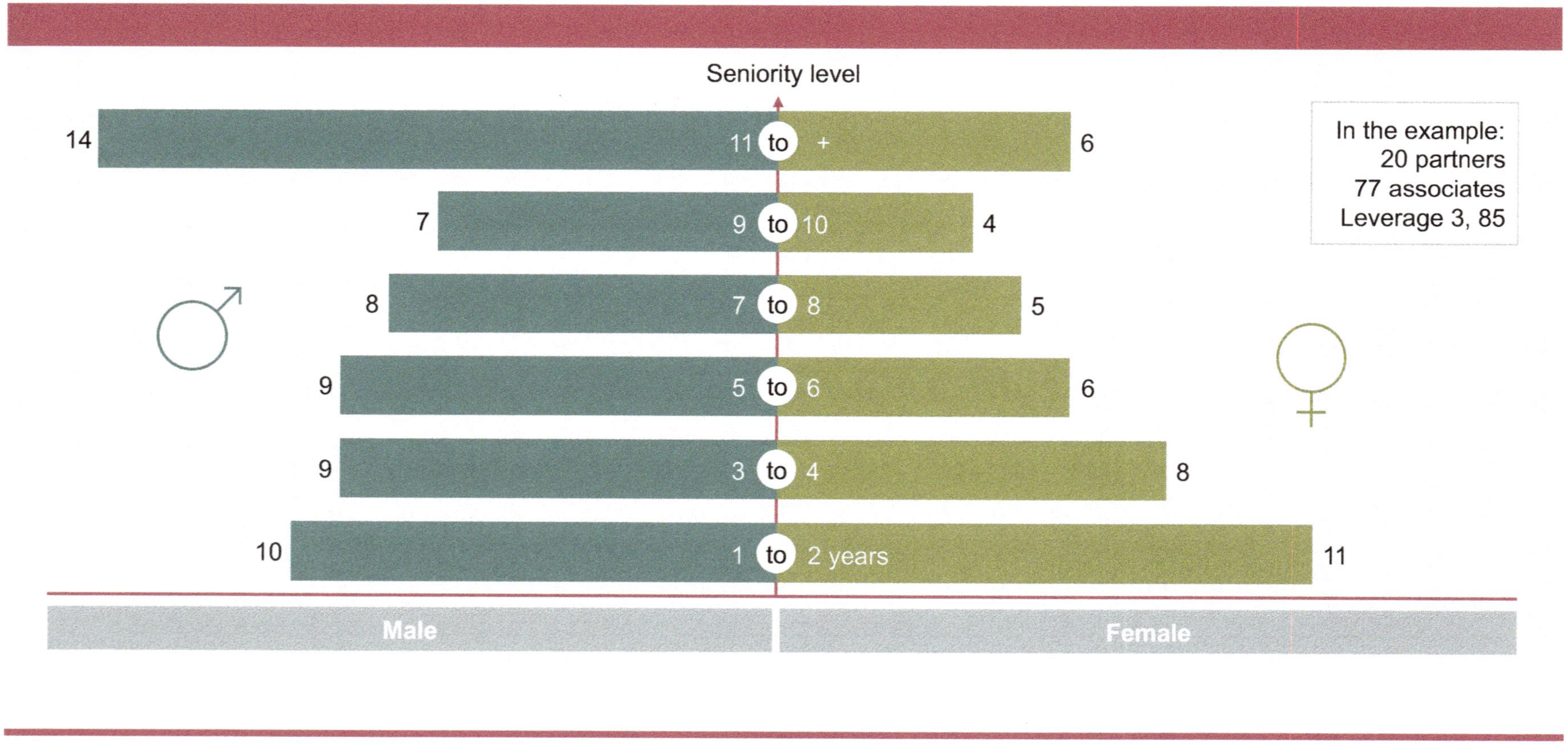

Source: Venturis Consulting Group, all rights reserved.

Figure 13. Developing a gender balance programme[70]

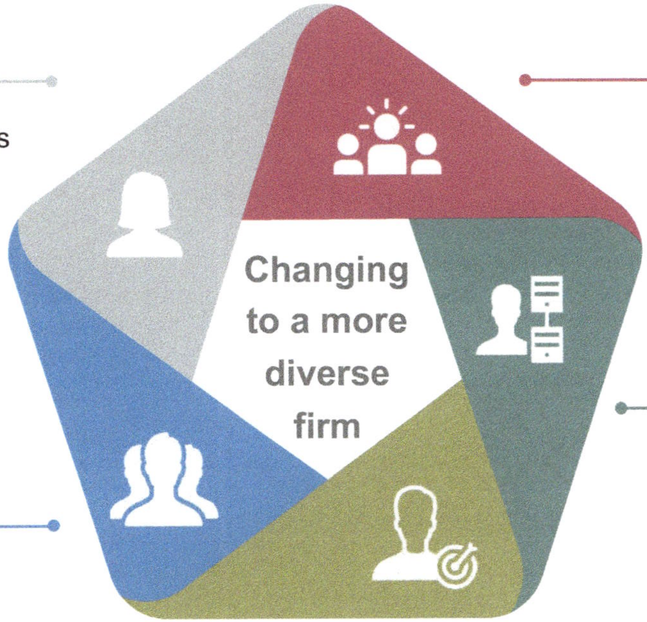

Equip women

- Create a talent pool
  - Keep gender diverse candidates until final recruitment stage
  - Widen the age frame to spot high potentials
- Support development
  - Training to increase influence
  - Organise mentorship and coaching programmes
  - Encourage networking

Change culture

- Raise awareness of lawyers about the different behaviours and the benefits of gender balance in a firm
- Develop practices for better work-life balance for all
- Reassure mid-level male lawyers

Engage top management

- Ensure board leadership
- Consider quotas for mixed representation at partnership and board

Adapt the rules of the game

- Develop non-biased performance criteria
- Break the cycle of linear career development and reward different experience

Define objectives and measure

- Define quantified objectives at all levels (recruitment, development, promotions to partnership)
- Include these criteria in lawyers' performance evaluation

Source: Venturis Consulting Group, inspired by Grandes Ecoles au Féminin (see n 70).

later than usual, to leave room for women – or men – who may have delayed their career for family or other reasons.

Define and monitor objectives: A proactive approach requires that quantified objectives be defined at all levels (recruitment, development, promotion to partnership) and included in partners' performance evaluation to measure progress in the composition of their teams.

Some law firms have started to adopt quotas. Quotas are largely unpopular, but can be an efficient method until gender-diverse teams have become the new normal.

The gender diversity strategies at Vinge are outlined in Case Study 5.

Case Study 5

Embracing diversity and inclusiveness

Maria-Pia Hope, managing partner and CEO, Vinge

> *Diversity is an important driver towards any sustainable version of the future. Vinge (which has 450 experts working in five offices) was the first Scandinavian law firm to set a diversity target. "We continue to fine-tune our holistic approach – not merely because responsible enterprise is a prerequisite for long-term success, but also because equal treatment and inclusiveness is the right path," explains managing partner Maria-Pia Hope.*

As a leading Nordic full-service law firm, it is paramount to ensure that our clients' success is powered by sustainable business legal advice. We believe in a working environment free from discrimination, where everyone can achieve their full potential and prosper professionally. This is why Vinge supports the development of current and future women leaders.

We closely monitor the number of women at each level of seniority. Tailored measures are put in place, such as leadership programmes, sales coaching and mentoring for high-potential women. Top talent with partner or counsel potential are identified on an annual basis. We also strive to shed light on all aspects of a senior law firm career, as external research has shown that women tend to overestimate what such a career involves in terms of input, while sometimes underestimating their own talent and aptitude. Talented women are matched with senior partners outside their practice area to serve as informal mentors and some participate in external mentoring programmes. Additionally, to level the playing field, we have revised our parental leave package with a view to actively encouraging men and women alike to take parental leave.

The firm's board of directors, as well as the senior management team, consists of four women and five men; the latter will change to five women and four men in 2022. The local managing partners are two women and one man; and in 2022, all will be female. In 2014, Vinge set a target to the effect that 50% or more of the new partners in the firm's partner intake in the next five years should be women, thereby mirroring the firm's entry-level recruitment. At the end of 2019, 42% of the new partners in the five-year period were women. We then set a new target with the same content for the next five years. As a combined result, the firm has as many women as men on partner track and 58% of senior associates are women.

In 2020, we were happy to receive the European Women in Business Law Award for the eighth time running as the firm which has best implemented equality throughout its operations in Sweden.

When recruiting, consideration is always given to the group demography. In cases where there is uneven distribution due to age, background, experience, personality or gender, we look to find candidates who can add diversity to the group. If there are several candidates for an available position, we choose the candidate who can best add to the firm's diversity, provided that the qualifications are otherwise the same.

We run a long-term *pro bono* diversity project focused on achieving greater diversity in terms of nationality in the legal profession. The project is conducted in close cooperation with select upper secondary schools in Stockholm, Gothenburg and Malmo in areas with high immigrant concentration, where we offer pupils everything from education to the possibility of working as a summer trainee. Several participants have since become lawyers and we have our first partner who started with us on the programme.

The following goals are followed up and documented on an ongoing basis, in the annual salary review as well as in internal cooperation forums, which include employees from across the firm:

- All operations shall be free from discrimination.
- All employees shall have equal rights and opportunities regarding work and opportunities to develop.
- The share of newly elected partners in the period to 2024 shall be 50% women.
- No one shall consider themselves discriminated against based on any of the grounds which constitute discrimination.
- No one shall feel harassed or bullied at the workplace, irrespective of what this may concern.
- No one shall consider themselves discriminated against during

the recruitment process or the appointment of positions, irrespective of whether the position is appointed internally or externally.
- Differences between salaries or terms of employment which are based on one of the grounds of discrimination shall not exist.

As we strive to be an organisation characterised by diversity and equality, we will continue to support all our women and men in growing and evolving as individuals in order to reach their full potential.

(b) Other diversities

Disability: In Western countries, businesses are often encouraged to recruit disabled people by law, sometimes through quotas; but businesses are not well equipped to respond to specific needs. The non-profit sector plays a major role in raising awareness and helping to reduce inequalities (and discrimination) in recruitment and career development. As an example, Droit Comme Un H,[71] based in France, is dedicated to helping talented lawyers with disabilities to access the legal profession.

Ethnicity: Some diversities are hard to measure, such as ethnicity, religion and sexual preferences, as different cultures approach them differently. Unlike in the United States, ethnicity cannot be tracked in several European countries – often by law – to protect people's privacy. In most international law firms, the variety of countries in which they have offices and the diverse cultures, qualifications and languages of their members reflect the variety of their people.

Religion: Likewise, the variety of religions represented in law firms cannot always be known or quantified. Respect for all religions is required in these organisations. Firms commonly take active measures to show openness and promote freedom of religion. Examples include:

- having an ecumenical dedicated prayer room in a quiet part of the office;
- organising religion and culture awareness sessions as part of their training; and
- ensuring that no retreats are planned on religious celebration days.

LGBTI+: Most international law firms have launched LGBTI+ programmes over the past five years. The right balance must be struck to ensure that these programmes can achieve their objectives. LGBTI+ people should feel welcome and listened to, without being judged, and should be able to talk openly about related issues. They should never be pointed at or required to disclose at any point. This is even more important in countries where LGBTI+ people face discrimination or prosecution.

To show their commitment, firms often sign public charters and develop their own internal programmes – involving dialogues, awareness sessions and language design elements – aimed at developing a more inclusive firm culture (eg, including defence of human rights in a *pro bono* programme).

5. Law firms expected to have their governance in place

The 'G' in 'ESG' stands for 'governance' – good governance. Governance is part of the broader concept of governance, risk management and compliance (GRC). Although law firms – as legal advisers – have always advised their clients on legal risks, until recently they were less focused on their own GRC infrastructure.

GRC-related issues are perhaps not the most compelling topics. Sustainability discussions quickly turn to the 'E' of sustainable environment and the 'S' of social responsibility; but without proper GRC infrastructure, the decisions made, the actions to be implemented and the goals to be monitored can quickly degenerate into "It could have been a success, but..."

GRC in law firms covers not only issues such as decision making, partnership structure and composition (eg, in terms of diversity) and partner remuneration, but also matters such as client and matter intake, the supply chain (ie, in terms of service providers and procurement), and local, national and international local bar rules and regulations (eg, know your client (KYC), money laundering and terrorist financing, and whistleblowing policies).

There are two main aspects to the importance of GRC. First, law firms are independent economic actors, like all other businesses, with their own responsibilities and obligations; second, law firms are increasingly confronted – or, more positively, encouraged – by broad stakeholder groups (from clients and employees to environmental and human rights organisations) to make ESG an integral part of their strategies. In that respect, and as we have seen, the importance of GRC cannot be underestimated.

The following sections do not set out a full and complete overview of GRC in law firms, but rather describe the interplay between this concept and ESG and sustainability.

5.1 Governance

Perhaps the most fundamental part of GRC is the governance

structure. If the governance structure – which includes the partnership structure and composition, profit distribution and remuneration, and decision-making processes – is not aligned with the firm's ESG strategy, it will become very difficult (perhaps even impossible) for the firm to walk the talk.

Long before the term 'ESG' as such was known in law firm boardrooms, firms were aware of the need for and value of D&I at all levels of the organisation, including the partnership. In other words, SDG 5 – "Achieve gender equality and empower all women and girls" – is often embraced as a core value, but a lot remains to be done at both partnership and board level.

As previously mentioned, law firms have their own obligations and responsibilities; and at the same time, clients, talent and other stakeholders have justified expectations of law firms. As such, law firms – ranging from niche and boutique outfits to international business law firms – are increasingly making it a strategic priority to adopt policies that promote D&I at all levels (including partnership and board level).

In addition to the justified goal of "empower[ing] and promot[ing] the social, economic and political inclusion of all, irrespective of age, sex, disability, race, ethnicity, origin, religion or economic or other status",[72] there is also a need to value a diversity of backgrounds. This leads to a variety of views, arguments and suggestions, based on which a partnership and the management board can take more balanced and informed decisions.

(a) Inclusive and informed decision making

Due to a combination of size and legal structure, in general, law firms are not legally bound by national D&I laws and regulations (where these exist). However, in response to demand from talent, clients and the changing composition of the workforce (white middle-aged men versus young women and men from different cultural and socio-economic backgrounds), law firms have become increasingly aware of the needs and added value of D&I. Although the goals that have been formulated in this regard may still be far off for many firms, policies are now in place that should result in greater diversity. Law firms in almost every market segment have embraced policies that should lead to the broadest range of constituents of different ages, genders, expertise and socio-economic backgrounds. This diversity should be reflected at all levels, from (junior) associates and business support staff to the partnership and the management board.

In practice, it is now increasingly common for women to be promoted as board members and managing partners; for the first time, a non-UK

"If the governance structure – which includes the partnership structure and composition, profit distribution and remuneration, and decision-making processes – is not aligned with the firm's ESG strategy, it will become very difficult (perhaps even impossible) for the firm to walk the talk."

citizen is the global senior partner of a large international firm;[73] and professionals from other sectors and industries with impressive track record at C-suite level are increasingly appointed as members of the management board.

International business law firms such as Pinsent Masons and Eversheds Sutherland[74] have adopted an interesting approach by appointing shadow boards – respectively called the Spark Board and Shadow Leadership – comprised of employees from various regions, practices and functions. Pinsent Masons' announcement of this development stated as follows:[75]

> *The average age of the members of the firm's two primary leadership committees, the Board and OpsCom, is 20–30 years older than the most common age group of the people in our firm. The Spark Board was born from a recognition that, whether you are a lawyer, a fee earner in another discipline or a specialist in an area of business operations, you can offer a different way of thinking and alternative expertise on the big issues. There is a recognition around our business that no single person or committee has the monopoly on good ideas, and that's where the Spark Board has a role to play. We can better use, and benefit from, the diversity of all our people.*

As we continue to transition our business we know our decision-making needs to be informed by the widest possible range of talents within our business. If we want our business to work better we have to be prepared to push a few boundaries and that includes around key decision making.

These initiatives – which are relatively easy to implement – support the promotion of innovative ideas (Eversheds Sutherland); and above all, they support an inclusive approach to strategic decision making, ensuring that the management board benefits from different perspectives from both outside and within the partnership (Pinsent Masons).[76]

(b) Shared value

The creation of shared value is a key element in assessing a company's sustainability. This involves creating benefits for the business and its shareholders as well as for other members of the company and for society at large.

But what is the meaning of 'shared value' in a law firm? It involves:

- creating financial value for partners and sharing this financial value in a transparent way;
- creating value for other members of the firms in an equitable way; and
- creating value for the communities in which the firm operates or for society at large.

Profit distribution and sharing financial value: Profit per partner is essential in evaluating the economic value generated by the firm and its benefits to its partners. However, this is not antinomic to sustainability. In evaluating a firm's sustainability, one must check whether the profit-sharing system is transparent and subject to objective rules. Questions may arise as to how partners' remuneration compares to that of associates and other employees – especially where a firm is seeking certification of some kind, as many certification bodies require that this gap be limited.[77]

Some firms have incentive or profit-sharing schemes under which employees receive an annual bonus linked to the firm's profitability in the previous year – an indication of the firm's willingness to share some of the value it generates.

Shared value in non-financial terms: Benefits for associates and other employees include not only remuneration systems (eg, how official and transparent a grid is; how employees can benefit from profit-sharing schemes), but also non-financial benefits (eg, receiving on-the-job training, gaining experience with emblematic clients, solving complex cases or benefiting from flexible working).

With regard to the benefits for society, firms are increasingly implementing policies to share value with their communities and beyond. For example, some firms are establishing foundations, financed by their partners, to support specific causes; or are setting up *pro bono* schemes to provide access to justice or training to those in need. However, shared value goes beyond *pro bono* work and donations.

Shared value involves rethinking the firm's activities so that they create value both for the firm and for society. For instance, imagine that a firm builds (or buys) a legal tech tool to streamline its activities and draft standard form agreements more quickly and reliably. It uses this to provide a quicker, more reliable service to clients, thereby increasing its profits and presumably sharing part of the value gained to reduce the cost for clients. It also uses the tool to identify new markets comprised of clients that need standard help and would otherwise be unable to access legal services. (In this case, the firm could gain a new source of profits based on a different model of low-cost, repetitive services that also bring real benefits for those most in need.)

"Profit per partner is essential in evaluating the economic value generated by the firm and its benefits to its partners. However, this is not antinomic to sustainability."

KPIs on created shared value: If a firm's leadership has embraced sustainability as a core principle of its strategy, then ESG criteria should be listed among the evaluation criteria for partners (as well as lawyers and other employees – see Part II, sections 4 and 5). In other words, partners should have a (financial) incentive to contribute actively to the ESG strategy and objectives.

ESG criteria could be measured through a quantitative assessment (eg, percentage of revenues generated by ESG matters; employee churn and burnout rates); and could be part of the firm's annual personal and professional business plan (including ESG topics, business development and know-how activities). A limited number of evaluation criteria and related KPIs and processes should be carefully selected and precisely stated, and should reflect the priorities of the firm's ESG strategy.

5.2 Compliance and risk management

Unlike governance, which has always been a fundamental part of the structure of law firms, risk management and compliance are relatively new concepts in the legal sector, to the extent that they relate to a firm's own operations and structure – let alone in the context of ESG and sustainability.

"A well-designed, well-executed risk management and compliance function supports not only the firm's regulatory framework, but also its reputation, its strategy in general and – more specifically – its ESG strategy."

The risk management and compliance function of a law firm serves – or should serve – more than just an administrative check-the-box purpose. A well-designed, well-executed risk management and compliance function supports not only the firm's regulatory framework, but also its reputation, its strategy in general and – more specifically – its ESG strategy.

Law firms are increasingly becoming gatekeepers. Irrespective of its strategy, a firm must have a structure in place that deals with regulatory requirements relating to issues such as conflict checks, KYC obligations, anti-money laundering, fraud and terrorist financing.

Depending on the firm's strategy, the risk management and compliance function is also increasingly responsible for assessing and ensuring compliance with:

- the policies that derive from the ESG strategy as formulated by the firm; and
- both binding and non-binding obligations that derive from rules, regulations and even charters at local, national, international and supranational levels.

The evolving role and responsibilities of the risk management and compliance function have internal and external elements. In terms of risks, opportunities and threats, it should take into account the interests of the law firm, including both client intake and reputational risk.

(a) Client intake

Lawyers have always had a choice as to whether to accept a client (or not). Today, the client intake process is no longer just an administrative exercise in terms of filing the client's details and conducting a conflict check. It has become a strategic decision: do the client, the type of work and the sector and industry fit with the firm's strategy and market positioning?

ESG has added a further layer to the client intake process, affecting risk management, compliance and strategic assessment.

Firms that have formulated a purpose and an ESG strategy cannot escape the need for a fundamental strategic discussion on:

- the types of clients they want to work for;
- the types of instructions they want to handle; and
- the sectors and industries they want to focus their business development and marketing efforts on.

Figure 14. Client intake

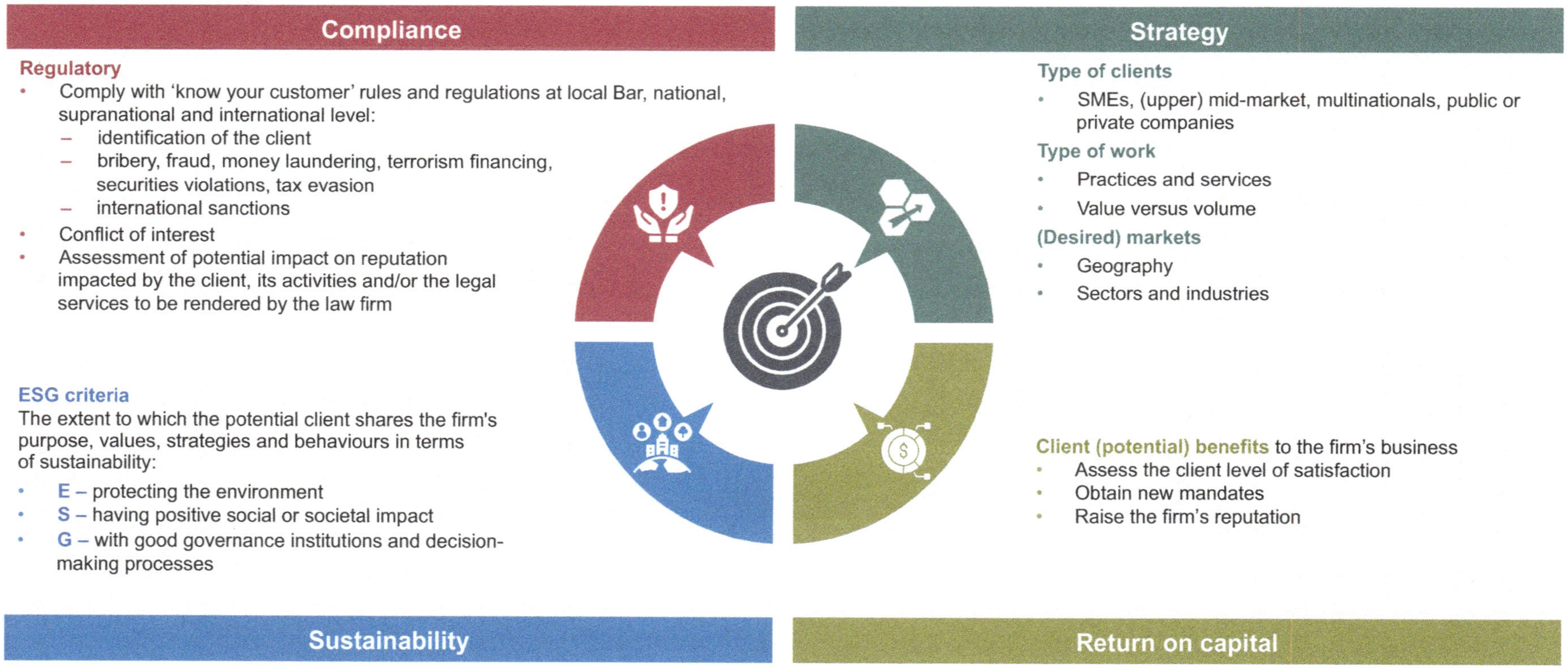

Source: Venturis Consulting Group, all rights reserved.

Moreover, ESG requires firms to go beyond mere compliance with their legal obligations (eg, KYC and money laundering), and to assess and comply with their obligations as derived from, for example, UN principles and treaties.

(b) Reputation

Another element that should be highlighted within the context of risk management is the growing importance of reputation. Until recently, the main concern for law firms in terms of reputation was the quality of their people and the legal services they provide to clients. When a firm has a good reputation, clients know that their interests are in safe hands. However, climate change, decreasing biodiversity and the erosion of human and labour rights and animal rights have put law firms under the microscope. While multinationals and financial institutions (eg, banks, pension funds and investment funds) have come under criticism from NGOs for some time, the latter have more recently broadened their scope to encompass the professional service providers that make clients' business possible from a legal, tax and accountancy perspective.

In order to assess reputational challenges, opportunities and threats, law firms must develop a framework and an organisational infrastructure that take into account not only the different types of clients and types of work, but also elements that relate to the firm as an independent economic actor with its own responsibilities, such as:

- long and stressful working hours and conditions;
- inappropriate behaviours;
- burnout rates;
- D&I;
- housing; and
- the firm's own supply chain (ie, its service and product providers).

In this context, law firms must develop and implement programmes that focus on issues such as:

- internal codes of conduct;
- personal and professional leadership;
- best practices;
- stakeholder management;
- media and press; and
- crisis management.

Firms that cannot sufficiently prove they have developed and are implementing an ESG strategy will undoubtedly face higher reputational risk. Also, they will need to start selecting clients and matters more strategically and with greater diligence.

5.3 Roles, tasks and responsibilities to sustain initiatives

The board's allocation of responsibilities around sustainability is key. In an ideal world, sustainability should not merely be a separate job, but rather a way of doing business for everyone in the firm. However, having a dedicated person or group of people to coordinate and pursue initiatives across the firm is essential in embedding sustainability in everything that the firm does – at least initially, until it becomes commonly accepted that sustainability is everybody's business. To promote this important and necessary cultural change, most organisations appoint a dedicated chief sustainability officer (CSO).

The CSO role is evolving and becoming increasingly important in larger firms. These professionals have a pivotal role to play in helping the whole firm to embark on its sustainability journey.

The role of the CSO, which is not yet standardised, requires diverse skills. Perhaps the most important are finely honed communication and coordination skills, to secure buy-in across the whole firm and ensure that everyone – from the board to each individual staff member – understands and acts upon the firm's sustainability strategy. One of the CSO's core missions is to understand, monitor and reduce the firm's negative impact on the environment, whether through its own activities or those of its supply chain.

6. A law firm's organisational and operational responsibilities

Earlier in this Special Report, we identified that law firms have multifaceted roles as:

- the legal advisers of their clients;
- business partners with an in-depth understanding of the complex sectoral issues around ESG;
- a bridge between society, policymakers and regulators and businesses; and
- independent economic actors.

ESG will ultimately compel law firms to take action on several fronts, such as with regard to clients, practices and sectors; but also, for example, with regard to talent management. We have further highlighted that without proper and functioning governance, risk management and compliance infrastructure, firms will find it very difficult, if not impossible, to implement and execute a successful ESG strategy.

This section focuses on operations – not in the sense of the core operations of a law firm (ie, providing legal advice), but rather the operational side of the organisation. In contrast to certain clients of

Figure 15. Key governance actors for sustainability

Board's ESG sub-committee	A sub-committee at board level helps develop the capabilities of a dedicated group and guarantees more availability and attention to the topic, as well as being the board's constant reminder that sustainability is at the heart of the firm's strategy.
Chief Sustainability Officer (CSO)[78] or Director of Responsible Business	The CSO, otherwise called Director of Responsible Business, is a key person to: coordinate all initiatives; ensure they are important strategic issues at the top of the agenda at board meetings; ensure that all stakeholders are aligned internally or externally; and ensure the firm's processes are in order and complied with. The CSO's mission is to steer the whole firm on its transformation journey towards sustainability, preferably reporting to the board, or its ESG sub-committee, as the direct owner of strategy. This reporting line is a clear indication that the board treats the topic seriously, and a key condition for sustainability to be embedded in strategy. In addition, it gives credibility to the CSO's role in conducting the implementation of the firm's strategy.
Inclusion or diversity partner	One of the first positions to appear in the CSR arena was the inclusion or diversity partner, sometimes supported by an officer. It is often a separate function in international law firms: D&I is treated as a distinct paramount issue.
***Pro bono* partner**	The position of *pro bono* partner, involving a practising partner to overview *pro bono* efforts across the firm, is quite common. Often, *pro bono* partners continue to practise their specialty and work mainstream for their paid-for matters. In addition, they supervise the opening of, and legal work on, *pro bono* matters, that are treated as standard business with regard to onboarding rules, conflicts of interest and ethical rules. To our knowledge, Hogan Lovells is the first firm to appoint, as a partner, a qualified lawyer fully dedicated to *pro bono*. *Pro bono* officers, as support professionals, ideally report to the *pro bono* partner, with a dotted line to the CSO.
Chief Development Officer (CDO)	In smaller firms, the CSO function can be delegated to the CDO: the CDO is likely to have the necessary qualities of a CSO. The CDO role is often quite central and requires good coordination skills. Also, sustainability becomes core to development, as clients often require evidence of the firm's involvement and actions in requests for proposals.
Chief Communications Officer (CCO)	The CSO role is sometimes delegated to the CCO.[79] The CCO's role is also central in the firm, as they interact with all other functions, and often report directly to the board. They are the first point of contact to be informed if a risk of crisis occurs. Also, an important part of the CSO role is

Continued on next page

Figure 15. Key governance actors for sustainability *continued*

	about communicating the firm's progress towards sustainability. Note that the roles of CDO and CCO must be clearly and separately identified, with distinct responsibilities and agendas. Sustainability must not be understood or dealt with simply as communications or development, to avoid the risk of this being perceived as mere 'greenwashing'.
General counsel (GC)	For law firms who have a GC, his/her role is paramount. Even if not appointed CSO, they are in a central position regarding the firm's ESG practices. In firms that do not have a separate CSO, the legal function is one that may have the remit to coordinate, support and develop the ESG strategy. GCs are uniquely placed to know of all potential ESG issues, as they collaborate with all departments and partners. They ensure compliance with business ethics, anti-corruption and anti-money laundering rules, oversee client intakes and protect against conflicts of interests. They are the ones to evaluate risk management and issues along the supply chain, and ensure that the firm navigates safely among the growing ESG regulations and norms. GCs must take part in the materiality assessment of the firm's positive or negative impact and in defining what the priorities should be in the firm's sustainability strategy. GCs are also asked to validate the firm's ESG report before publication, to prevent any disclosure risks. This responsibility is important and should not be left to the last minute as the risk of liability, whether reputational or judicial, becomes real.
Align other heads of functions	Dedicated positions are key to support CSOs and to ensure coordination, strategic focus and implementation throughout the firm. All heads of departments should be involved (HR, business development, communications, compliance, IT, etc ...).

Source: Venturis Consulting Group, all rights reserved.

law firms – such as the agribusiness, fossil energy and fashion industries – law firms as such are not known for having a big impact on the environment. However, given the global objective of reaching net zero by 2050, all businesses – including law firms – must aim to achieve this goal themselves. This also requires them to take responsibility for matters such as premises, catering, travelling, office supplies, waste, energy, IT and the supply chain.

There are numerous reasons why firms should conduct a review of their organisation and operations, and develop policies that will make them more responsible and sustainable, such as those relating to:

- reputation and credibility (ie, walking the talk);
- financial performance (ie, cost savings); and
- people and talent management (ie, facilitating the needs and preferences of employees to strengthen loyalty).

The actions to be undertaken and the policies to be implemented by firms could relate to a variety of steps to reduce carbon emissions, such as:

- managing energy consumption;
- reducing travel;
- engaging in the '3 Rs' (ie, reducing waste, reusing materials and recycling) – particularly in relation to paper and IT hardware; and
- participating in carbon offsetting programmes.

6.1 Sustainable ('net-zero') objectives

To help meet the global objective of the 2015 Paris Agreement,[80] law firms are increasingly committing to reduce greenhouse gas emissions in order to achieve net zero emissions by 2050 or sooner.[81] The challenge involved in this undertaking is to benchmark against official calculations, in order to ensure that all emissions are captured and progress is accurately monitored. To this end, firms are applying science-based targets.[82] They are primarily opting for a combination of reduction measures and compensation (or offsetting) policies for those emissions that cannot be directly reduced.

Law firms are also increasingly involved in achieving net zero objectives. The recent Net Zero Lawyers Alliance, founded in June 2021 by 20-plus international business law firms (see Figure 7), is a legal sector coalition aimed at accelerating the path to net zero. The founders of the coalition have positioned themselves as collaborators rather than competitors on this global issue, "where we'll either all win or all lose".[83]

The sixth IPCC report, prepared in the run-up to the COP26 conference in 2021, demonstrates unequivocally that:

- human activity is responsible for climate change;
- world temperatures will have increased by a minimum of 1.5°C (compared to pre-industrial levels) by the 2030s;
- the frequency and intensity of extreme conditions (fires, floods, heatwaves) will increase; and
- sea levels will rise higher than anticipated.

Stabilisation is possible through a drastic reduction of human carbon dioxide (CO_2) equivalent emissions.[i]

After numerous attempts by different actors, the Paris Agreement was the first to set a global framework to avoid the risk of climate change by keeping planetary warming below 2°C (compared to pre-industrial levels). The high level of greenhouse gases (GHGs) in the atmosphere is the principal cause of global warming, the main driver of climate change, with CO_2 representing 65% of total GHG emissions. Reducing carbon emissions has thus become a key priority and led to the inspiring EU Green Deal in 2019. This established a roadmap to achieve carbon neutrality by 2050, involving all actors – including private sector businesses – and encouraging sectoral initiatives.

Although law firms are responsible for lower levels of GHG emissions than many players in other industries, all companies (and individuals) must play their part; and law firms can take numerous steps to improve their carbon footprints.

i IPCC Sixth Assessment Report, www.ipcc.ch/assessment-report/ar6/#:~:text=The%20IPCC%20is%20now%20in,to%20its%20latest%20Methodology%20Report.

Given the scope of this Special Report and the fact that carbon reduction and offsetting programmes require specialised expertise, we limit ourselves here to describing the main sources of carbon emissions for law firms and how they can be reduced, including by:

- managing energy consumption;
- reducing travel;
- engaging in the '3 Rs' (ie, reducing waste, reusing materials and recycling) – particularly in relation to paper and IT products and devices; and
- participating in carbon offsetting programmes.

(a) Buildings and energy

A law firm's offices and its heating, lighting and air conditioning systems are its main source of energy consumption and GHG emissions. Many firms are now seeking to reduce their energy usage to become more environmentally responsible, enhance their reputation and credibility, and save on costs. Methods that are commonly used throughout the legal sector include:

- installing motion sensor lights;
- reducing use of heating and air conditioning systems, and using them more efficiently;
- turning off computers in the evening and weekends;
- using efficient LED lightbulbs;
- switching to green (sustainable) energy suppliers;
- renovating and insulating old and/or unsustainable office buildings; and

"While office buildings are now well insulated and CO_2 emissions are minimised, individual homes where staff work remotely tend to be less energy efficient, and firms must take this into account when calculating their footprint."

- relocating to green or sustainable office buildings (eg, French business law firm Gide moved its Paris headquarters to a fully renovated office building, certified as *haute qualité environnementale*).[84]

A relatively new challenge that firms pursuing net-zero objectives must address concerns the recent increase in remote working. While office buildings are now well insulated and CO_2 emissions are minimised, individual homes where staff work remotely tend to be less energy efficient, and firms must take this into account when calculating their footprint.

(b) Travel

For most business law firms with a substantial international practice, travel is the second-biggest source of carbon emission. Firms have had travel policies in place for some time now, primarily related to travel budgets, car hire and business class or economy flights. Given the greater awareness among law firms of the need to become more sustainable, they are now including sustainable elements in their travel policies by:

- promoting sustainable means of travel (eg, cycle plans, public transport subscriptions, electric cars);[85]

Figure 16. The '3 Rs' model adapted to law firms

1

- Avoid buying goods that are 'over packaged'.
- Re-use items such as scrap paper, postal packaging, boxes and packing cases.
- Avoid unnecessary printing costs:
  - Install double-sided photocopying machines, or produce double-sided documents whenever possible.
  - Install a code for printing only when a lawyer is waiting at the photocopier (to avoid a pile of unallocated documents waiting at the photocopier).
- Avoid disposable items such as plastic cups and provide mugs and glasses instead.
- Buy products made from recycled materials such as paper.
- Turn off equipment when it's not being used. Turning lights off can reduce the energy used by 25%; turning off computers at the end of the day can save an additional 50%. Include energy saving automatic motion sensors.
- Replace outdated, inefficient electrical equipment with energy-efficient equipment and keep equipment running smoothly.

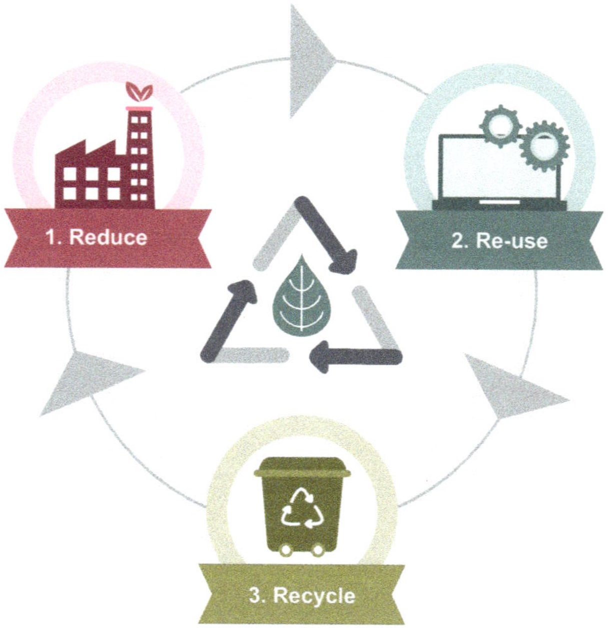

2

- Re-use containers, packaging or waste products.
- Donate unwanted office furniture and equipment to charities.
- Check whether goods can be repaired rather than replaced.
- Use rechargeable rather than single-use batteries and ask your local council about how to dispose of them properly.
- Engage with suppliers who can take back packaging for re-use.

3

- Separate your recyclables such as glass, plastic, paper and metal from other rubbish – depending on what your local council will collect.
- Recycle waste material into useable products where possible.
- Buy recycled goods – these have already saved resources and raw materials and helped reduce the overall quantity of waste.

Source: Venturis Consulting Group, all rights reserved.

- setting clear guidelines on short-distance journeys (eg, high-speed train journeys rather than flights);
- reducing or cancelling avoidable travel (eg, virtual meetings via Zoom or Teams rather than physical meetings);
- optimising travel plans (ie, requiring a minimum number of meetings per journey); and
- using a limited number of travel agencies that share the firm's sustainability values and provide reliable data on CO_2 consumption.

(c) Reduce, re-use, recycle

Many of the topics discussed in this Special Report require decision making at the strategic level and may entail a radical shift in strategic priorities (which is worthwhile, but not always easy!). But law firms can begin reducing the amount of waste they produce almost instantly, without any significant changes in strategy. By carefully managing the waste it generates, a firm can contribute positively to what is called the circular economy:

> *The circular economy is a model of production and consumption, which involves sharing, leasing, reusing, repairing, refurbishing and recycling existing materials and products as long as possible. In this way, the life cycle of products is extended ... This is a departure from the traditional, linear economic model, which is based on a take-make-consume-throw away pattern. This model relies on large quantities of cheap, easily accessible materials and energy.*[86]

So what does this mean for law firms? First, law firms are already doing a lot to promote the circular economy. They usually have policies in place to reduce waste and to facilitate recycling through separate waste collection (waste reduction is preferable to recycling). These policies save costs and are integral to responsible supply management.

The main type of waste that law firms generate is paper. In this context, many law firms are seeking to go paperless through smart use of technologies (ie, by avoiding printing, filing and storing hard-copy documents).[87] A well-managed paperless office facilitates significant reductions in both paper and storage space. Younger lawyers in particular now take notes online and store them in their electronic archives. Timesheets and invoices are now prepared and submitted or shared online. To avoid the need to print out a draft when reviewing a contract, firms are providing lawyers with a second screen for their desks. This even applies to marketing materials: event invitations are now generally digital and brochures are less commonly used, even if they have not yet been fully abandoned.

(d) Managing the carbon footprint of technology

Developments such as the paperless office and remote working have been made possible by technology. As such, technology has become an enabler for many trends and advances in law firms, from practice management, client service delivery and collaboration (eg, digital meetings by video conference) to know-how management (eg, digital libraries). But the increased importance of technology in today's business environment also presents new challenges, which directly relate to ESG issues.

In developing an ESG strategy, a firm cannot ignore the environmental impact of its technological platform (ie, hardware and software, such as computers, laptops, smartphones, tablets, cloud solutions and software applications). While technology has major advantages, drawbacks include the following:

- Computers, and especially cloud computing and online video conferences, require massive amounts of energy and thus generate significant GHG emissions.
- Cloud computing also requires significant storage capacity in large data centres, for which acres of valuable land are needed.
- Computers and smartphones incorporate heavy metals such as mercury, lead, beryllium, cadmium and dioxins. These heavy metals are often extracted under conditions that have a negative impact on the workforce, the environment and local communities.
- The useful lifespan of a computer is three to five years and that of a smartphone just 2.5 years. This relatively short lifespan results in huge volumes of e-waste.
- Due to the increase in both the number and severity of data security breaches and the growing number of data regulations (eg, the EU General Data Protection Regulation), law firms must increasingly integrate IT security and compliance into their overall GRC management.

It might be tempting to replace employees' 'old' iPhones with the latest model, install state-of-the-art IT infrastructure or give everyone a tablet for Christmas. However, firms that have embraced sustainability as one of their core principles must consider the impact of their technological infrastructure and ask searching questions in this regard: "How can we develop the most sustainable IT infrastructure?" "Do we need to replace our computers and smartphones? What should we do with the old ones (eg, recycle them or donate to charities)?" "Can we switch to a more sustainable provider (eg, Fairphone)"?[88]

(e) Carbon offsetting

Given the Paris Agreement targets, activities that cause carbon emissions should be minimised or avoided altogether. However, we do not live in an ideal world; and despite our best efforts and intentions, business activities will still end up causing carbon emissions. For this reason – and for the same reasons that they develop policies to reduce energy, travel and waste – law firms are also increasingly implementing carbon offsetting programmes.

Firms can either:

- offset their own emissions against unused emissions of a third party (although this is not the preferred solution); or
- capture their carbon emissions through carbon sinks (eg, by planting trees).[89] In this context, reforestation is often used by law firms to ensure that, for example, a partner conference is carbon neutral. In order to avoid greenwashing, firms must ensure that such projects are executed by professional organisations (eg, Trees for All), and are measured and audited by third parties.

6.2 Supply chain management, responsible procurement and referrals

As with many significant developments in the international legal market, clients are a main driver of the transition to sustainability. Law firms have a lot on their plate as they seek to implement ESG-related practices, enhance D&I and become more responsible and sustainable organisations. On top of these day-to-day tasks, they are also increasingly required to manage their supply chains in a responsible and sustainable manner – in the capacity of both legal service provider and purchaser.

(a) The law firm as a responsible legal service provider

Supply chain management for law firms is now a significant element in their relationships with clients. Firms are no longer expected merely to deliver sound legal advice; they are also expected to deliver in terms of:

- well-being, work-life balance and D&I;
- proper GRC infrastructure; and
- sustainable (net zero) operations.

Clients that need to both comply with international ESG rules and regulations and maintain their market reputations are increasingly making sustainable policies and reporting a condition of engagement.

In practice, this means that firms must be able to develop and present extensive data on, for example:

- their carbon footprint;
- codes of conduct regarding relationships with employees and other stakeholders;
- percentage of female partners and associates;
- health and security measures; and
- waste and energy-saving measures.

Firms which cannot deliver on these elements and which poorly manage their supply chains – including their own organisation – may eventually lose their licence to operate.

Clients may require endless reporting factors. However, the questions asked and the KPIs expected are not harmonised from one firm to another, making it difficult for clients to interpret and compare them. The process can be very time and resource consuming, both for the supplier and for the client. This data is sometimes too difficult for medium-sized businesses (ie, most law firms) to prepare and too complex for clients to analyse. This is why organisations such as EcoVadis[90] provide standardised rankings.

(b) The law firm as a responsible purchaser

However, law firms are not just subject to the supply chain management policies of their clients; they are also increasingly developing

"Law firms are not just subject to the supply chain management policies of their clients; they are also increasingly developing procurement policies for their own (service) providers."

procurement policies for their own (service) providers. There are various reasons why firms should engage in procurement management, including reputational, financial and organisational reasons. To this end, firms should develop internal and external infrastructure that enables them to be responsible purchasers, including by:

- setting clear and fair delivery and payment conditions;
- providing necessary training to support teams;
- promoting a culture of dialogue with suppliers (ie, what firms can reasonably expect from their suppliers and vice versa); and
- developing clear processes to ensure respectful behaviours.

(c) The law firm as a referrer of business (referral strategies)

Another interesting component of a law firm's supply chain is the role of law firms in providing work to each other (inbound and outbound) – better known as 'referrals':

> *An international referral strategy focuses on the development and maintenance of an international network of law firms and other professional service providers, facilitating a profitable stream of inbound and outbound work that fits with the core clients, the core practice and sector groups, and the core value of the work ... firms need to be able to refer the cross-border work of their clients to a 'safe pair of hands'. Firms that can do so have a competitive advantage over peer firms that have no such or restricted capabilities.*[91]

The growing importance of ESG in legal practice will also have an impact on how firms should develop and structure their international referral strategies, to ensure that partners share not only the right expertise and competencies, but also the same ESG culture and priorities.

To conclude, the following takeaways may be highlighted regarding supply chain management:

- Law firm clients are increasingly demanding ESG guarantees from their law firms. As legal service providers, and hence part of clients' supply chains, law firms are expected to have their own organisations and operations in order.
- Law firms must act as responsible purchasers and be reasonable in the conditions they impose on suppliers; and
- Law firms must actively monitor their supply chains in order to ensure that supplier malpractice or misconduct does not have a (negative) effect on their reputation and credibility.

These takeaways also fully apply to referral relationships between firms.

The role of sustainability rating agencies

Many clients now require that their legal advisers and how they monitor their supply chains be rated by third-party rating agencies – whether NGOs or businesses such as EcoVadis (https://ecovadis.com). The latter is the market leader in supply chain evaluations and the most commonly used agency in the legal profession.

Its sustainability assessment includes:

- a customised questionnaire, including an audit and 360-degree analysis;
- a scorecard and rating;
- a performance benchmark; and
- a review of the firm's practices regarding the environment, work relations, human rights, ethics and responsible procurement.

The rating is continually evaluated over time and the agency can advise on how to improve. The rating is a helpful guide for all businesses, including small to medium-sized companies, and for law firms.

A large number of law firms (eg, Clifford Chance, Gide, Linklaters, Hogan Lovells, Blake Morgan) are rated by EcoVadis at the request of their clients. According to Clifford Chance:

> *Increasingly clients require firms to disclose their sustainability measures and practices. As participants in the UN Global Compact, and with a long-standing commitment to support the Sustainable Development Goals, we have a strong foundation, but we are ready to work with our suppliers and clients to build on this. The work we're doing with EcoVadis is really helping us and enabling us to articulate and report against the ESG commitments we have made.*[i]

i Clifford Chance, "Introducing a new carbon action module to measure Clifford Chance's supply chain", 19 July 2021, www.cliffordchance.com/insights/resources/blogs/responsible-business-insights/2021/07/introducing-a-new-carbon-action-module-to-measure-clifford-chance-supply-chain.html.

7. Strategy, positioning, differentiation – and their alignment

We have previously discussed the many elements that inform the formulation and development of a sustainability strategy. A long-term ESG effort can provide a true competitive advantage for law firms, but only if it is included in the strategic agenda, goes beyond day-to-day organisation and is implemented successfully.

Law firm leaders must develop and implement strategies in a fast-changing business environment characterised by high levels of volatility, uncertainty, complexity and ambiguity. In doing so, they must avoid numerous traps, such as:

- 'boiling the ocean' (ie, having endless meetings, discussions and analyses without getting to the real strategic issue);
- ignoring the crucial trade-offs between strategic options (ie, not making real choices); and
- focusing on the operational side of things, instead of the strategy itself.

Firms that truly aspire to have a sustainability strategy should realise that this is about:

- making difficult choices regarding clients, practices, sectors and work;
- securing the buy-in of all stakeholders (eg, partners, associates, business support professionals, clients);
- implementing transparent and inclusive governance systems;
- attracting and retaining talent who increasingly choose to join and remain in a firm on ESG grounds; and
- avoiding greenwashing or social washing.

Becoming a sustainable law firm involves transforming your business model – not only to avoid negative impacts, but also to create an overall positive impact on society and thus maintain a competitive advantage in the long run.

One simple yet powerful way to analyse and visualise your business model holistically and strategically is to use the famous Business Model Canvas,[92] adapted to include the impacts of the business, whether positive (revenues) or negative (costs)[93] (see Figure 17 overleaf):

1. Begin by describing your client base and your client segments.

2. For each segment, you have a value proposition – that is, the clients' needs that you fulfil through your key activities.

3. Your key activities are the services you need to perform well to meet your clients' needs.

4. Your development means are the ways in which you approach your clients and the touchpoints to convince them to use your services.

5. Client relationships are the types of relationships that you develop with your clients, and how you acquire and retain them.

Figure 17. Sustainable business model canvas for law firms

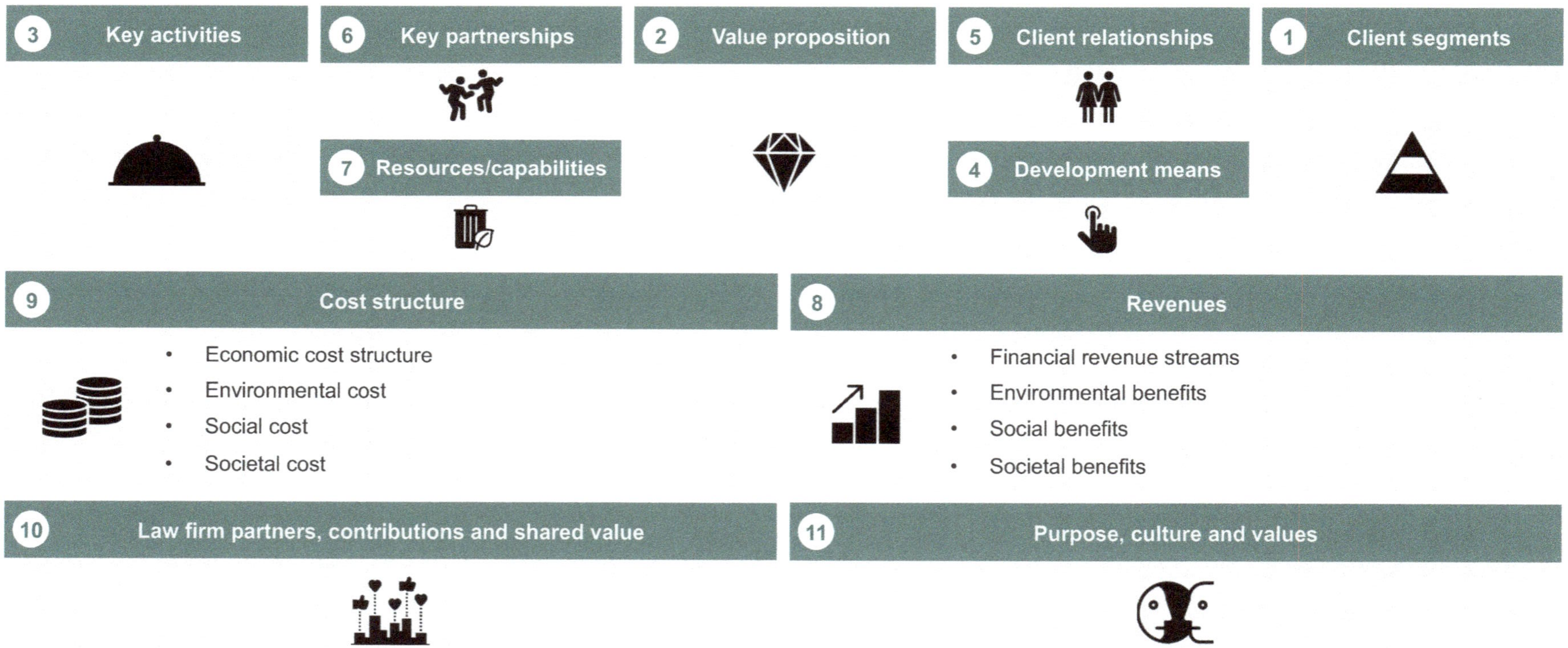

Source: Adapted from Business Model Canvas, Pigneur and Osterwalder, and Business and the SDGs: A Framework for effective corporate Involvement, Rob van Tulder (see n 92).

6. Pay particular attention to reviewing partnerships that you rely on to leverage your business model.

7. Key resources and capabilities that are indispensable to your business model will assist you in drawing up a list of stakeholders that are crucial to your business (eg, suppliers, subcontracting lawyers, external partners).

8/9. In describing how your revenue streams are generated, the sustainable Business Model Canvas invites you to document both the economic value and the social, societal and environmental impact – whether positive or negative – generated by your law firm. The economic value depends on the pricing methods and financial revenues generated, minus the costs incurred to support that economic value. Other revenues and costs will include your law firm's positive and negative impacts, both on the environment and on society.

10. The firm's partners are not only owners but also producers of the value generated by the firm, and decide on how this value will be shared with wider stakeholders.

11. Their purpose, culture and values, according to which they operate together and which guide their decisions, complete this holistic business model description.

The original Business Model Canvas assumed that the business was mainly profit driven for its partners. The sustainable business model assumes that the profit value proposition "also includes a social and environmental purpose" and a broader value proposition. This is why Venturis Consulting Group, in adapting the model to law firms, feels it is important to articulate the purpose, culture and values that unite the partnership and inspire its business strategy.

This model is helpful in understanding how each element should interrelate and align with the others towards realising the value proposition (centre of the model) offered to clients and society (right side of the model) thanks to resources and partnerships (left side of the model). Gaps and duplications will quickly become clear and give management ideas on how to adapt their strategy to develop a more sustainable law firm.

There is no single correct way to approach the sustainability transformation in a strategic way. Before suggesting a methodology, we share a 'real-life' case study which reveals the approach to sustainability transformation at Vieira de Almeida.

Case Study 6

Setting the standards for sustainable success

Paula Gomes Freire, managing partner, Vieira de Almeida

Vieira de Almeida (VdA), a leading Portuguese law firm with 460 people in seven jurisdictions, incorporates ESG into every aspect of its strategy, with a focus on technology as a key driver of change.

CSR and its positive impact on society have been embedded in VdA's DNA and core values ever since the firm's creation. We believe that as lawyers, our conduct must be anchored in rigorous ethical and decency values, and responsibility towards our community and ecosystem. The firm is a pioneer on the Portuguese legal market, having formalised a CSR programme more than 13 years ago.

VdA and the Vasco Vieira de Almeida Foundation – established in 2016 with a mission of citizenship education – provide *pro bono* legal assistance, citizenship education and third-sector capacity building. Through the firm's Green Project – a sustainable development and eco-efficiency programme (see further below) – VdA monitors its carbon footprint and is committed to minimising the firm's negative environmental impact.

Given the unprecedented times since the outbreak of the COVID-19 pandemic and the dramatic changes that can already be perceived in society, VdA – fully conscious of the challenges ahead – is fully committed to strengthening resilience and ensuring a sustainable future for the firm.

In 2020, we launched a strategic plan for 2021–2025, called "Setting the Standards for Sustainable Success". This was the beginning of a new learning curve of sustainable development. VdA is determined to embrace new challenges and remain ahead of the game while respecting its legacy and protecting its culture.

CSR and having a positive impact on society are part of VdA's history and core values. Hence, our strategic plan, launched during a global pandemic, aimed to weave ESG into the firm's core and embed it not only in our strategy, but also in management decisions and the practice of law.

Purpose

VdA undertook a thorough and thoughtful process involving its people, clients and other stakeholders in order to spell out its purpose. VdA is committed to respecting its legacy and protecting its culture, and will continue to embrace its role in society and fulfil its responsibilities by putting know-how and expertise at the service of clients, and by playing an active role in finding solutions to the social and environmental problems that we all face as a society.

Clients

VdA is well prepared to advise organisations on long-term value creation and to assist clients with the increasingly complex ESG issues they face. To this effect, VdA has launched an ESG Integrated Services Platform – a cross-practice platform that aggregates the offer of ESG advisory expertise and promotes cross-staffing and collaboration between different practice areas.

People

At VdA, we truly believe that our sustainability is increasingly dependent on our ability to nurture an environment of trust, with strong shared values and sense of engagement, while promoting D&I and the well-being of the team. With one-third women in the partnership and a diverse talent pool, we recently adopted the global United Nations Women's Empowerment Principles and joined the UN Target Gender Equality project.

During the pandemic, we increased flexibility for remote working and launched the We4Wellness programme, fostering the well-being of our people by addressing mental and physical health issues.

Our staff are encouraged to contribute their time to *pro bono* work – we spend more than 8,000 hours on providing *pro bono* legal services annually – and to actively participate in several CSR initiatives, creating a strong sense of citizenship and engagement with the collective effort to strengthen our contribution to the community.

Operation

Twelve years ago, VdA established the Green Project with a view to promoting not only a culture of awareness of the importance of this issue, but also of effective action, focused on minimising the environmental impact of our activities and achieving carbon-neutral status in the long term. We deepened our commitment to reducing carbon emissions by consuming electricity exclusively from renewable sources across all our facilities and implementing sustainable mobility solutions (eg, charging stations for electric cars, electric bicycles and scooters available for employee use).

We increased our ambitions with regard to the SDGs and were among the first 600 organisations worldwide to adhere to the United Nations' SDG Ambition programme, an accelerator initiative that aims to promote better and more rapid integration of the SDGs into companies' management (including systems and processes).

Technology

Fully conscious that technology is a key driver of disruptive change in any business, VdA recently promoted an intensive debate with reputed academics and experts on the likely impact of technology on businesses across sectors. The conclusions of this debate were presented in a book called *Sustainable Success: The Future of Technology, Leadership and Culture*, which compiles insights, commentaries and predictions on how technology will impact on work, leadership and culture within organisations; and in particular, on how law firms and their leaders will have to adjust to this new world if they want to succeed.

Part III: How to engage in transformation – our approach to sustainability in law firms

From the preceding discussion, we are now aware of our responsibilities as lawyers and the importance of sustainability in every sense of the word; but how do you design and implement an ESG strategy in practice?

At Venturis Consulting Group, we have developed a practical tool that encompasses the elements of the SDG Compass[94] (a comprehensive "guide for business action on the SDGs"),[95] and that aims to help law firms in designing or reviewing their sustainability strategy. In Part III of this Special Report, we discuss the various steps and actions that firms can take to become truly sustainable. The process of designing and implementing a sustainability strategy depends on many factors, such as:

- market positioning;
- size;
- types of clients, matters and sectors/industries;
- financial structure; and
- governance model.

In other words, there is no such thing as one size fits all!

Figure 18. A practical model to make ESG an integral part of your firm's strategy

"Taking responsibility is changing the core of your operations"

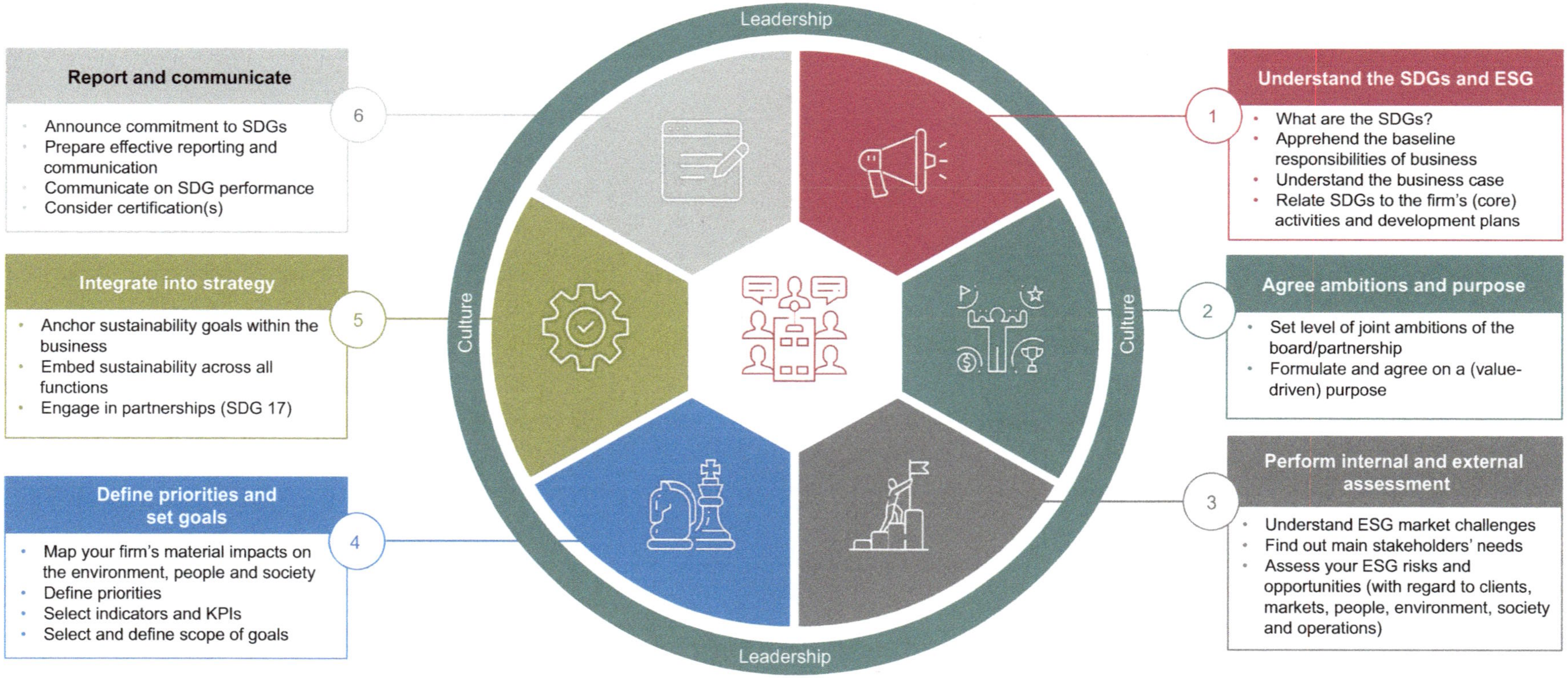

1. Understand the SDGs and develop a sustainability mindset

The first step on your sustainability journey is to embrace the SDGs. Study the 17 goals and the associated targets to understand the challenges and how they interrelate, as well as the global ambitions behind them. Try to relate these goals to your own law firm and consider a few objectives to which you as an individual or your organisation could contribute.

Part I of this Special Report discussed the phenomenal achievements of the United Nations in successfully calling all countries and economic actors to engage in the "2030 agenda for peace and prosperity for people and the planet", as reflected in the 17 SDGs.

Consider your firm, review its current business model and imagine how contributing to the SDGs could:

- nurture clients and talent;
- open up new markets or create innovative new opportunities;
- save costs;
- prevent risk; and
- positively impact profitability.

Understand that in the long run, your agenda must produce a positive overall impact on the 3 Ps: people, planet and profits. Having gained a general understanding of what is at stake, here is our step-by-step approach to setting your firm on its sustainability journey.

2. Agree ambitions and purpose

Once a firm (ie, leadership and the partnership) has determined in detail what sustainability, ESG and the SDGs are and what they could mean for its business, the partners must identify their joint ambitions and aspirations.

2.1 Evaluate partnership ambitions

Top-down involvement of the board and the partnership is paramount to the success of any strategic project, let alone a journey towards sustainability. First and foremost, the partnership is key in setting the ambitions of the project.

If the partners lack the personal motivation to invest the necessary time and effort in this project, the starting point should be to identify a small group of change champions who can seed a better understanding of sustainability challenges among the partnership. This will build the solid foundations which are necessary for the successful execution of an ESG strategy.

If the firm has a purpose, the partners should put it at the centre of their discussions. If the purpose needs adapting or if the firm has no purpose, this is the ideal opportunity to engage the partnership – and subsequently the whole firm – in defining the firm's purpose.

2.2 Develop a sincere, value-driven purpose

To be effective, a purpose cannot be decided unilaterally at the top level or imposed on the wider firm with no discussion. Defining a purpose is a lengthy process, in which lawyers exchange ideas and discuss the firm's values and culture, and then draft proposals on what they stand for. First drafts will be challenged and rewritten in a reiterative, cooperative way, until a single sentence is agreed in which every word has profound meaning.

The process should be as inclusive as possible:

- Start with the board. Prepare a storyboard to convince and engage across the wider firm and propose first potential drafts.
- Then engage partners. Encourage discussions. Initially, some partners may stay silent due to scepticism, lack of time or misperceptions about the possible impact of a purpose.
- Then involve lawyers and business support professionals, who will need to digest what the purpose means for them and how it might resonate in or apply to their day jobs. Share and record stories that illustrate the different points of the purpose, to make it as concrete and relevant as possible. Everyone should feel encouraged to challenge the draft purpose until it is finally approved.

Involving everyone – whether through workshops, retreats, online discussions and platforms or similar – will motivate and encourage them; and will ensure that they all know and understand the purpose, engage with it and hopefully apply it in practice.

The effectiveness of the purpose can be assessed from the extent to which it is supported and lived by firm members, and from their ability to articulate how it relates to them individually.

While you are discussing your firm's purpose, start analysing where your firm stands with regard to corporate responsibility.

3. Assess where you are, internally and externally

Once the partners have agreed on their joint ambitions and aspirations, a thorough qualitative and quantitative analysis must be conducted to assess the firm's capabilities, competencies and capital. This should relate to aspects such as the following:

"Once the partners have agreed on their joint ambitions and aspirations, a thorough qualitative and quantitative analysis must be conducted to assess the firm's capabilities, competencies and capital."

- organisation;
- people;
- clients, practice and sector groups;
- financial performance;
- (international) network and supply chain;
- business support; and
- governance model.

It should seek to identify what and where the firm can invest, and what resources are available to help achieve its sustainability goals.

In determining what is required for a firm and its respective practice and sector groups to develop a sustainability strategy at client level, questions such as the following should be answered:

- What types of clients do you serve and who are your core clients?
- What kind of work do you do for these clients?
- What are the main business activities and business centres or geographies of your clients?
- In which sectors and industries do they operate?
- What are the ESG challenges, opportunities and threats for these (core) clients, and in these sectors and industries?

- How important is each client to your firm (in terms of revenue and profit contribution, but also in terms of reputation)?

3.1 Review market and global standards requirements

This assessment should also include the following elements, which require special attention when designing an ESG strategy:

- Look at what your clients and peers are doing and you will see that most have already started out on their journeys – even if only slightly or without a clear ESG strategy. Involvement varies across the spectrum, from accepting *pro bono* work to identifying several SDGs as key objectives or putting sustainability at the heart of the firm's strategy and being rated as such.
- Identify the main criteria that define a sustainable firm. A self-assessment audit is a good way to determine what sustainability means in practice and to assess where you are. Two useful references are:
  - ISO 26000,[96] the only international norm that provides directions on environmental and social responsibility to entities, associations and enterprises of all sizes. It offers a method to implement CSR in organisations and is very helpful for law firms. VIGO is the first French law firm to be evaluated on ISO 26 000;[97] and
  - the B Corp Impact Assessment tool,[98] which was developed for B corps – businesses that are legally accountable to balance profit and purpose. Their social and environmental performance is verified and communicated publicly. The tool provides free, easy-to-use questionnaires that cover all areas to work on in order to become a positive impact company.

With these requirements – and your law firm's own position – in mind, seek to understand how your firm is perceived by, and interacts with, its main stakeholders.

In the global legal sector, around 50 law firms (out of 3,500 corporations) are B Corp certified. B Corp law firms have put sustainability at the core of their strategy and have an overall positive impact – whether societal (eg, they target underprivileged clients or those most in need), environmental (eg, their core and only practice is environment), or social (eg, their employees are part of their governance). Interestingly, these are mostly small to medium-sized firms. They are mostly US firms; only a handful are European, although those which were certified most recently (Swiss, Spanish and UK) may be starting a new trend.

3.2 Select and interact with stakeholders

Stakeholders play a crucial role in the development of an ESG strategy. Formulating a purpose; gaining an in-depth understanding of what clients require from a firm in terms of practices, operations and D&I; entering into partnerships (SDG 17); managing the firm's supply chain – all of these actions require interaction with stakeholders.

The stakeholder concept was first developed by Edward Freeman in 1984.[99] CSR extends beyond a firm's immediate shareholders and partners to encompass allies and beneficiaries – essentially, all parties that interact with the firm. Stakeholders beyond immediate partners are those people who contribute to the firm's activities, whether directly or indirectly; and on whom the firm's activities have an impact, whether positive or negative.

Primary stakeholders include employees, clients, subcontractors and suppliers – parties with which the firm has entered into direct contractual relationships. They are easy to identify. More distant stakeholders are those that are impacted by the firm's activities (eg, the bar association or law society, the media, neighbours, government and local authorities, legislators, industry bodies, NGOs) or that could benefit positively from the firm's activities (eg, those most in need who do not have access to education or the law).

Identify and map the most important stakeholders for your firm. Then identify those stakeholders with which you interact most frequently because:

- they are essential to your activity;
- they have been vocal in challenging your activities and you need to understand why; or
- they have a good vision of the market and care about your firm's progress.

Figure 19 (overleaf) sets out an example of an initial map of stakeholders for a law firm, before they have been prioritised.

Listening to stakeholders will increase your awareness of potential risks for your firm and the expectations of third parties, and may even create new opportunities. Your decisions will be better informed if you manage this process sincerely.

Rank your stakeholders' importance to your business, listen to their concerns and prioritise their issues. This process is necessary to anchor your sustainability strategy in reality and to work on making a positive impact for stakeholders as well as for your business.

Figure 19. Map of stakeholders

Partnership stakeholders

- Suppliers
- Subcontractors
- Other lawyers
- Media
- Notaries, bailiffs
- Auditors and accountants
- Professors and researchers
- Universities and students

Internal stakeholders

- Partners
- Associates
- Service professionals

Client stakeholders

- Sectoral groups
- Client organisations
- Individuals

Justice-world stakeholders

- Court judges
- Administration
- Legal society and Bar
- Independent/sector regulatory body
- Parliament – regulators

Society stakeholders

- NGOs
- Activists
- Local associations
- Local authority officials
- Neighbours and surroundings
- The most in need

Source: Venturis Consulting Group, all rights reserved.

(a) Engage in sincere dialogue
Adopt a sincere and transparent approach in consulting your stakeholders, listening carefully and leading constructive discussions to find more balanced ways of doing business.

(b) Prepare topics and objectives
Before approaching your stakeholders, set clear objectives, prepare the dialogue and identify the themes to focus on. Aim to end up with a few key issues which will have a significant impact on stakeholders while also being actionable for the firm. As a business, your firm needs to generate profits as well as creating value for society and preserving the environment. Outcomes should be balanced, win-win solutions.

(c) Choose adapted dialogue methods
Firms must choose the right method to achieve each of their objectives. Law firms are becoming quite imaginative in engaging in dialogues and conversations with their two main stakeholders:

- associates and employees – whether through one-to-one meetings, online open discussions platforms, suggestion boxes, working groups and even plenary sessions at global retreats; and
- clients – making the most of client feedback programmes, whether through online surveys or qualitative interviews.

Law firms must also engage in dialogue with their suppliers (as responsible purchasers, exercising their duty of vigilance), and with society at large (including activists).

(d) Revert and explain
Asking for input and engaging in dialogue with stakeholders will raise expectations. Participants will expect feedback on the results of the consultations and on next steps. There is no need to make false promises; be transparent and sincere on where you are in the process and the main issues you are working on. Dedicated feedback for different categories of stakeholders will be appreciated. More general 'non-financial' reports on progress will be useful here (see Part III, section 6).

Firms that have a genuine intention to listen to stakeholders and to manage their risks proactively can use this as a true differentiator. They will make better-informed decisions and focus on real expressed needs. They will have more motivated stakeholders and generate more innovations and opportunities.

4. Define priorities and set goals
The next step is to identify clear objectives and priorities to set your ambitions and plan the extent of your transformation journey.

4.1 Analyse materiality and prioritise your SDGs

Review those issues that are important both for your law firm's business and for its stakeholders. Rather than drawing up a list of all issues together with the contemplated actions and programme, it may be helpful to position ESG topics on a map or visual matrix, to better highlight the priorities. In defining your priorities, consider the risks that ESG issues can have on the firm's business, as well as the material impacts – positive and negative – of the firm on the environment, people and society.

Figure 20 provides an example of a materiality matrix, illustrating a law firm's key priorities.

Irrespective of whether your firm has a CSO function, the materiality analysis should be carried out in close collaboration with the heads of each key function, to ensure that:

- all of the firm's issues are considered and prioritised;
- buy-in is secured from every function; and
- sustainability is integrated into the strategy of each function (see Part III, section 5.1). For example:
  - the business development function can feed back on clients' expectations with regard to sustainability, and can positively engage in green marketing and articulate to clients the financial and non-financial benefits of sustainable services; and
  - the communications function will be involved in preparing the ESG annual report (called the "Communications on Progress" report for firms that follow the Global Compact reporting rules),[100] and will have to walk the thin line between transparency and publicity (on reporting, see Part III, section 6).

Therefore, materiality assessment and prioritising must involve key stakeholders and functions to ensure that the programme is realistic and achievable. Targets and KPIs can only be assessed by taking account of relevant stakeholders and functions.

4.2 Develop targets and KPIs

What gets measured gets done. You need a starting point in figures to be able to see where you already have greatest impact and identify where your efforts will be most fruitful.

Measuring ESG is made more difficult by the lack of common standards, although organisations are now working towards a globally accepted framework for non-financial sustainability reporting. The European Taxonomy,[101] the Global Reporting Initiative[102] and other attempts to translate qualitative efforts into quantified monetary equivalent costs or benefits are all steps in the right direction.

Figure 20. Materiality matrix

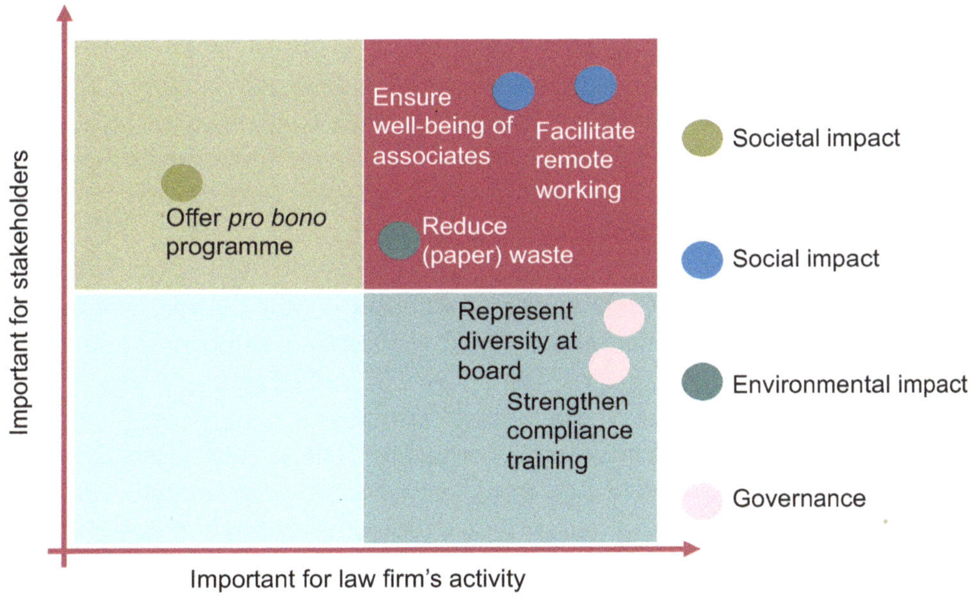

Source: Venturis Consulting Group, all rights reserved.

In the meantime, metrics and progress reports must be as accurate as possible. Quantified metrics are numerous and varied, depending on how each law firm wishes to make an impact. There can be as many metrics and KPIs as there are activities or law firms. Each firm should consider which are most appropriate to monitor its progress effectively and transparently.

(a) Set KPIs and track progress

The quality of measurement is crucial: a few simple, clear objectives can be tracked; but numerous fuzzy and varied objectives cannot.

As with any strategic effort, you must choose your priorities carefully and be able to let go of some potential objectives. As an interesting example, in its 2019 Communication on Progress for the United Nations, White & Case focused mainly on SDG 16 (57% of its activities).[103]

Be transparent on progress from one year to the next – not only on KPIs on the date of reporting. Sustainability is an evolving process – a journey, not an end point. For instance, some law firms leave all their Communications on Progress on their website in a reporting archive, so that stakeholders can track progress.[104] Some law firms also chart their progress on each objective on a visual continuum.

A non-exhaustive list of KPIs included in law firm reports is presented in Appendix 1. Only adopt those KPIs which will allow you to measure an objective that is important both to your firm and to its stakeholders. Keep it simple and material!

(b) Measuring your carbon footprint

Start-ups, NGOs and associations have designed numerous tools across different sectors to help individual companies to calculate their carbon footprints. For example, in the United Kingdom, the Legal Sustainability Alliance has designed a tool to help members calculate and track their carbon emissions.

In general, measurements are not easily comparable and not extremely accurate. The market is hoping for official measuring methodologies. On 28 October 2021,[105] the Science Based Targets initiative announced the first-ever global standard for carbon neutrality, with the certification of six corporates. The standard aims for decarbonisation of 90% to 95% of emissions before 2050, with the definition of short and long-term objectives along the way. Hopefully, this will lead to more standardised methods and objectives.

5. Align sustainability and strategy

So, the partnership has a keen understanding of the true significance of sustainability; the joint ambitions and aspirations have been agreed and formulated; the whole firm feels enlightened by its newly articulated purpose; leadership and management have obtained in-depth insight on the firm's capabilities, competences, capital and market positioning; and three to five strategic sustainable priorities have been defined for each respective practice and sector group and business support function. It is now time to implement the strategy and embed sustainability across the whole organisation.

5.1 Embed the SDGs within the business

The firmwide sustainability strategy should be translated for each practice and sector group and business support function (eg, HR, business development, communications, facilities, IT) into three to five strategic sustainable priorities, with explicit (underlying) objectives which are measurable based on clear KPIs, and which will be carried out according to the strategic action plan (SAP).

Each of these steps should be based on:

- the purpose of the firm;
- the (potential) positive or negative impact against the three ESG elements; and
- contribution to one or more SDGs.

Figures 21–23 present examples of concrete priorities, objectives and actions at different levels of the firm.

Figure 21. Strategic priority at firm level

Aligning the governance model with the firm's ESG strategy ('form follows substance')

Objective	Strategic action plan	KPIs	Responsibility	Timing
Stimulate sustainable activities and (desired) behaviour of partners (as role models) which make a positive contribution to the desired positioning and the execution of the strategic priorities of the firm.	• Analysis of the effectiveness of the current partner performance system and the profit-sharing model. • Based on the results of this analysis, the current profit-sharing model may be adjusted in order to stimulate implementation, integration and connection of ESG ('best') practices and between partners and teams.	**Performance model** • Percentage of total revenues and profits generated by ESG clients and matters. • Time spent on ESG product and team development.		
Develop and stimulate implementation, integration and connection of joint: • ESG practices; • ESG clients; and • best practices between partners and teams.	Develop an ESG decision-making framework and appoint an ESG partner and/or ESG steering group with clear roles, responsibilities and tasks.	**Decision making** • Number (or %) of shared ESG clients. • Best practice methodologies. • Number of ESG programmes developed.		

Source: Venturis Consulting Group, all rights reserved.

Figure 22. Strategic priority at practice and sector group level

Improvement of the (non-)financial-economic performance of the practice and sector groups in relation to their ESG services offering

Objective	Strategic action plan	KPIs	Responsibility	Timing
By [year], [25%] of the revenues generated by the [practice/sector group] directly relate to ESG legal services.	• Agree on the definition of ESG legal services in terms of types of clients, work, sectors and industries. • Introduce a billable hour and revenue target for ESG matters per fee earner and/or per practice group.	• Revenue per lawyer and per partner. • Profit per lawyer and per partner. • RULES*.		
• Develop ESG clients and matters. • 'Refine' the client portfolio.	• Perform qualitative and quantitative client portfolio SWOC** assessment for the top 25 clients. • Identify and eventually say goodbye to clients and/or types of work that do not fit within the ESG focus of the firm and practice group. • Adapt the client onboarding process.	• Type of clients. • Type of work/matters. • Retention rate. • Revenue per client. • Number of new clients. • Reputation of the client (eg, Net Promoter Score, social media rates).		

***RULES**: Realisation, Utilisation, Leverage, Expenses, Speed ****SWOC**: Strengths, Weaknesses, Opportunities and Challenges

Source: Venturis Consulting Group, all rights reserved.

Figure 23. Strategic priority at organisational level

Alignment of the internal organisation with the ESG strategy and market positioning of the firm

Objectives	Strategic action plan	KPIs	Responsibility	Timing
• Increase the involvement of all people in the firm to contribute to the implementation of the ESG strategy. • Stimulate sustainable initiatives, activities and operations throughout the firm.	• Organise roundtable sessions (ie, stakeholder engagement) to develop concrete action plans on how the firm as an organisation could further contribute to sustainability (eg, reduce waste such as paper and plastic, introduce carbon offsetting schemes, introduce meat-free lunches, offer healthy snacks). • Introduce a simple annual business operating plan, in which financial and non-financial ESG objectives and activities are aligned with the overall ESG strategy of the firm (on personal, practice group and business support level).	• Number of sessions organised and stakeholders involved. • Amount of waste and energy produced and saved. • Carbon footprint. • International certification (ie, ISO 26000, B Corp).		

Source: Venturis Consulting Group, all rights reserved.

5.2 Collaborate and enter into partnerships

The task ahead of us is so immense that it is essential to take action in the ways that will have the greatest impact. This will often involve entering into partnerships with specialised organisations to make the most of each other's capabilities. While a firm can offer training and legal assistance, it does not have the capacity to find those who need it. Associations on the ground will know networks, situations and how best to contact people in need in developing regions.

But this is easier said than done. No one questions the power of successful collaborations and partnerships to achieve ambitious objectives, as long as all ingredients are in place to ensure success.

(a) Partnership projects need time and involvement

Often, firms are tempted to pursue pet projects or philanthropic projects, as these are quick to implement. In entering into partnerships, however, hard work must be invested in finding the right partner; understanding how it works, its strengths (eg, less organised but more flexible) and its objectives; and identifying how each partner can build on the other's strengths to respond to need and create value both for themselves and for society.

"The task ahead of us is so immense that it is essential to take action in the ways that will have the greatest impact. This will often involve entering into partnerships with specialised organisations."

(b) Focus on one or a few well-chosen partnerships
Because of the time, effort and learning curve involved, it is paramount to concentrate on a limited number of projects. Time and resources are limited, and it is only by building trust and progressing up the learning curve that impactful results can be achieved. Focusing on too many initiatives at once will be counterproductive.

(c) Understand the win-win potential of value creation for both parties
Preparing for a partnership project is an intensive and thorough process. The firm must identify a partner that will benefit from its core activities and ensure that it can make the most of the partner's capabilities. Choosing the right partner is essential; as is cultivating a deep understanding of how value will be created for both parties. As a result, partnership projects are generally slower to get off the ground; but with the right preparation, they can be sustainable in the long run.

6. Report, communicate, review, improve
Finally, the firm should communicate what it is doing to all stakeholders. Reporting is the final step in the ESG strategic transformation loop.

Some large law firms are now required to report by law. This is the case for LLPs under UK law and corporates of a certain status and size in EU jurisdictions, based on the game-changing EU Non-financial Reporting Directive. New CSR reporting regulations are under discussion and will likely require smaller businesses to connect financial and non-financial reporting in order to develop more comprehensive, transparent and comparable reports. We can also assume that voluntary reporting will be the norm for those law firms that are not legally required to report; and that non-financial reporting standards will become increasingly comparable and compulsory for all institutions.

6.1 Draft the report
One major advantage of reporting is that it requires a firm to set out in writing its current situation, set goals, consider its achievements so far and outline the overall impact of its initiatives. Articulating these different elements enhances awareness and understanding of the firm's real impact. This is a powerful tool both for the reporting team and for the wider ESG team. Reporting is also used externally to demonstrate the firm's achievements as a responsible business, often at clients' request.

Firms use different norms and guidelines to measure and report their sustainability efforts. Global firms often choose to focus on a number of SDGs. Those firms which are signatories to the Global Compact – an initiative to help businesses become a force for good – must prepare an annual sustainability report according to the guidelines set out in the Global Compact Communication on Progress[106] or other internationally recognised standards (eg, the Global Reporting Initiative[107] or ISO standards).

The main issue is that as yet, there is no precise common standard for non-financial reporting. Many efforts are underway to improve this situation, such as the European Taxonomy. But until a detailed approach to quantify efforts has been standardised globally, reporting approaches will remain varied and comparisons between firms will be difficult.

The content of these reports will also vary. Often, firms' annual reports include details of *pro bono* projects or tell positive impact stories that will speak to the hearts of stakeholders. Some highlight the processes in place to improve sustainability. The best reports also include details of the law firm's negative impacts and its actions to improve or overcome them; and share details of KPIs measured and achieved.

Case Study 7 highlights research that demonstrates not only the benefits of partnerships, but also the varied reporting methodologies.

Case Study 7

The case for sustainability reporting

Stina Warnstam Drolet, head of sustainability, Oxford Analytica; and **Isabella Bunn**, senior adviser, Oxford Analytica

Founded in 1975, Oxford Analytica is a geopolitical analysis and advisory firm drawing on a worldwide network of experts to advise clients on strategies, operations, policy and investments. ESG issues, in their wider economic and political context, have long featured in its work and are now taking a new direction.

Today, given the powerful reframing of ESG factors, we are redeploying our expertise in risk assessment, scenario planning, stakeholder mapping and policy analysis in innovative ways. We value the synergy with the emerging ESG responsibilities of legal advisers, including corporate counsel and law firms.

A major shift is underway in the field of ESG and sustainability reporting, demanding the attention of various professional services providers. At Oxford Analytica, we monitor issues such as:

- reporting standards;
- due diligence and disclosure mandates;
- reputational risk;
- litigation trends;

- investor and NGO activism;
- the changing role of corporate boards; and
- the impact of artificial intelligence in ESG information management.

Our recent collaboration with multinational professional services firm Ernst and Young Global Limited (EY) underscored an important lesson: the field of ESG is not just about risks; it is also about rewards, including long-term value creation for both business and society.

Earlier in 2021, EY approached Oxford Analytica to produce a thought leadership report on the fast-changing ESG landscape. EY wanted to help people understand the current state and trajectory of sustainability reporting and related policy.

We signed off the engagement in March 2021, after which our in-house team pulled together insights from our worldwide network of experts. We also conducted interviews with thought leaders across the policymaking, business and civil society sectors, and delivered workshops with EY leaders and subject-matter professionals, before sharing our findings.

In June 2021, we published a far-reaching 32-page report, *The Future of Sustainability Reporting Standards: The Policy Evolution and the Actions Companies Can Take Today.*[i] It provides a detailed and timely exploration of policy evolution in sustainability reporting and includes five key recommendations for companies to prepare for emerging sustainability reporting requirements.

Reflecting the significant changes underway in sustainability standard setting and reporting, the content covers the whole landscape of sustainability reporting standards. It details the progress that has been made over the past 18 months on standard setting as well as developments to come. For example, the International Financial Reporting Standards Foundation launched the International Sustainability Standards Board at COP26 with the aim of introducing a minimum global framework for sustainability-related financial reporting standards.

Our global expertise has allowed us to set our findings within the broader political context and consider the influence of a diverse set of actors, ranging from individuals to public and private institutions, which play a salient role in shaping the sustainability landscape.

i EY and Oxford Analytica, *The Future of Sustainability Reporting Standards: The Policy Evolution and the Actions Companies Can Take Today*, June 2021, www.oxan.com//media/3316/ey-the-future-of-sustainability-reporting-standards-june-2021-1.pdf.

6.2 Provide information; avoid greenwashing

By communicating its achievements to stakeholders, a firm can demonstrate its engagement and explain how it is contributing to society and the environment. Communication also serves as a kind of guarantee to the world at large that the firm is indeed contributing as described and is working to improve its positive contribution. However, the content of the report must be transparent and honest.

False or exaggerated representations can easily be perceived by stakeholders as 'greenwashing' – that is, false assertions that the firm is acting for good. This may trigger negative perceptions among employees or clients, causing them to lose trust in the firm. Highly visible firms also run reputational risks. As lawyers know, litigation based on false communications in ESG reports is on the increase.[108]

To avoid misrepresentation, try to be as objective as possible, with indisputable figures. Labels, ratings and third-party certifications are also helpful in this regard.

6.3 Gain credibility through certification

Certification is a way to help embed CSR in a firm's strategy and its day-to-day implementation, as well as to assert credibility in communications.

Different methodologies and approaches can be adopted in this regard – for example, evaluation according to ISO 26 000 or becoming a certified B Corp. Numerous other norms, labels and rankings that guarantee different aspects of CSR may be more important for your firm (eg, certification about the energy efficiency of office buildings or health and safety; best place to work rankings).

Depending on which aspects of CSR are prioritised in their strategy, law firms may seek to give their efforts added credibility. Appendix 2 presents some examples of different initiatives in this regard (guidelines, standards, labels, ratings, rankings, distinctions and certifications).

Conclusion

1. Do you still have objections?

This Special Report was finished during the Christmas holidays of 2021 – a turbulent year in many ways which reminded us once more that we are on the brink of irreversible change:

- The European Union announced its Green Deal;[109]
- A Dutch court ordered Shell to reduce the aggregate annual volume of all CO_2 emissions into the atmosphere (Scope 1, 2 and 3) resulting from its business operations products by at least net 45%, relative to 2019 levels, by the end of 2030;[110]
- Netflix released the documentary *Breaking Boundaries: The Science of our Planet* by Sir David Attenborough and scientist Johan Rockström about the collapse of the Earth's biodiversity and how this crisis can still be averted;[111]
- The UN COP26 climate conference was held in Glasgow; and
- The 10 most costly weather disasters caused damage worth more than €150 billion – over €17.5 billion more than the previous year. The damage caused by natural disasters (eg, floods, storms and wildfires) has been increasing for decades due to climate change.[112]

But this Special Report is not just about the roles and responsibilities of law firms in relation to climate change and declining biodiversity; it is about taking responsibility as a core principle of doing business that goes beyond the letter of the law. Lawyers' main duty is to represent the interests of their clients in both the short and long term. Clients' financial and business interests increasingly depend on the interests of their stakeholders and on those of society at large; as such, clients are no longer just pursuing (or expected to pursue) their own interests and those of their shareholders. This is where lawyers have a particular responsibility (and competency); and – perhaps even more convincingly – this is where the business opportunity lies. A client may have the law on its side, but what does this mean for its reputation (and for your firm's reputation)? What is the direct and indirect impact of its (legally permitted) activities on customers, employees, suppliers and the environment?

We strongly believe that sustainability is a global trend that is fast reshaping national and international legal markets; it will eventually have a profound impact on the strategies, operations and market positioning of law firms. However, the complexity of the issues it encompasses – the relationships between the SDGs; the technicality of carbon footprint calculations; the amount of non-billable hours involved in understanding the impact of ESG on clients' businesses; the balance between the firm's business and financial interests and sustainability – may also deter law firms from taking proper action.

But by making sustainability an integral part of its strategy, a firm can develop a clear and winning competitive advantage. Sustainability can make a positive contribution to:

- employee satisfaction and retention;
- client attraction and loyalty;
- risk prevention and cost reduction;
- the development of new markets, product and services; and
- ultimately, revenues and profits, and the firm's long-term sustainability.

In conclusion, our main tips for firms embarking on their sustainability journey are as follows:

- Keep it simple and avoid overengineering.
- Start with the most obvious measures and do things step by step:
  - Identify what your firm is already doing and what you could do more of, at both the organisational and operational level (eg, see Figures 21–23). For example, in terms of your carbon footprint, first identify the emissions that your firm is causing both directly (Scope 1) and indirectly (Scope 2), where you consume the most energy and what causes the most

"As with the tragedy of the commons, ESG concerns everyone; but we need serious incentives to stop looking to others to act and start proactively taking responsibility ourselves."

emissions; and then consider the impact of your supply chain. Your biggest negative impact is likely to be caused by your premises and business travel.
    - There is no need to be comprehensive, exhaustive or precise at the beginning.
- Identify where your firm can have the greatest impact (including at the client and practice level). Law firms are particularly well placed to contribute to:
    - SDG 4 (quality education);
    - SDG 5 (gender equality);
    - SDG 8 (decent work and economic growth);
    - SDG 10 (reduced inequalities);
    - SDG 13 (climate change);
    - SDG 16 (peace, justice and strong institutions); and
    - SDG 17 (partnerships for achieving the SDGs).
- Act! As with the tragedy of the commons,[113] ESG concerns everyone; but we need serious incentives to stop looking to others to act and start proactively taking responsibility ourselves.

Either we all win or we all lose.

Appendix 1
Examples of indicators

Below are examples of KPIs found in existing non-financial reports prepared by law firms, for inspiration.

1. Business and processes

1.1 Products and clients

- Reduced or increased number of matters, or fees generated by matters, that do or do not comply with the firm's objectives (eg, avoid advising on the establishment of a coal plant; growth and percentage of advice on clean energy matters; percentage of advice on matters helping the transformation towards cleaner energy (eg, green bonds)).
- Size and results of the firm's human rights practice.
- Size and results of the business integrity group, advising clients on integrity and alignment with the SDGs.
- Extent of support to social enterprises and NGOs as part of associate training, together with clients.
- Size and results of the firm's social finance and impact investment practice group.
- Size and results of the firm's green investment practice group.
- Number of clients working on the firm's *pro bono* matters.
- Number of collaborations/hours volunteered with clients.

1.2 Processes

- Conflicts and compliance (eg, number of teams; number of cases cleared).
- Anti-money laundering procedures.
- Anti-corruption and anti-bribery procedures.
- Risk management anticipation and reviews.
- Data protection processes.
- For all of the above, number of training sessions proposed/made compulsory and take-up within the firm.

1.3 Suppliers

- Declarative feedback or more thorough research to ensure that suppliers (including subcontractor law firms) are presenting the same level of guarantees as the firm.
- Rating agencies.

1.4 Purpose and culture

- Employee satisfaction surveys.
- Reputation (eg, reputation index, rankings, client quotes and survey results).
- Innovation.

1.5 Governance

- Election/appointment processes.
- Diversity on boards and among employee representatives.
- Collective decision-making processes, idea generation mechanisms etc.

2. People

- Turnover, attrition, coupled with entry and/or exit interviews.
- Learning and development opportunities.
- Quantitative KPIs of means deployed:
  - number of learning programmes;
  - hours dedicated to training (sessions and take-up);
  - average hours of training per full-time equivalent (FTE) per year;
  - ratings of training sessions by participants;
  - number of online/in-person training sessions;
  - legal/business training; and
  - number of *pro bono* matters recognised as skills enhancement (through partner-led, client-focused and properly resourced teams).
- Quantitative or qualitative descriptions of objectives achieved (eg, practice group created and developed; number of qualified experts).
- Well-being and resilience programme and associated measurements.
- Respect in the workplace policies and reporting mechanisms (number of actions/reports).

- Regular internal staff survey results.
- Certifications and rankings (eg, best place to work).
- Diversity.
- Nationalities, ethnic origins etc (NB this is illegal in some countries).
- Gender balance:
  - percentage of women promotions to partner;
  - percentage of women in partnership;
  - number of diversity/gender bias training hours;
  - signing of diversity charts; and
  - equal pay policy.
- Certification (eg, Mansfield Rule;[114] signing of diversity charters).

3. Community

- Firms will have different programmes in place to bring benefits to their communities.
- Most themes involve issues such as:
  - access to law;
  - reduced inequalities;
  - access to education; or
  - promotion of the rule of law and ethics.
- Objectives generally relate to the number of working hours devoted to citizenship causes (skilled volunteering by anyone in the firm) and *pro bono* cases (by lawyers) or fundraising.

KPI can include:

- sums raised by firm members, matched by firm management;
- number of hours worked *pro bono* by lawyers and in kind by all staff, quantified in monetary equivalent;
- the results of specific programmes (eg, number of children accessing education thanks to a programme);
- number of people helped over the year;
- number of employees sitting on the boards of charities or non-profit NGOs; and
- number of *pro bono* mandates.

4. Environment

Measures can be linked to global norms and to factors such as the following:

- percentage reduction in CO_2 equivalent (defined technically) (eg, reduce Scope 1 and 2 emissions by 5% from 2017 baseline per FTE by 2021);
- High Environmental Quality certification for buildings;
- ISO 14001 accreditation for environmental management systems;

- health and safety rules;
- reduced energy consumption, motion sensor lights and computer shut-offs;
- limitation of travel; bike-to-work programmes;
- reduced waste/water consumption; reduced use of paper and disposable bottles; increased recycling of paper and e-waste; composting; recycling days; and
- improved employee awareness and engagement (eg, number of campaigns to raise employee awareness; number of people taking part in contests; employee survey results).

Appendix 2
Examples of important initiatives (guidelines, standards, labels, ratings, rankings and certifications)

Sustainable Development Goals

- United Nations, Department of Economic and Social Affairs, Sustainable Development: The 17 Goals, https://sdgs.un.org/goals.

Social impact

- Mindful Business Charter, www.mindfulbusinesscharter.com.
- ISO 45001 Occupational Health and Safety, www.iso.org/iso-45001-occupational-health-and-safety.html.
- Great Place to Work®, www.greatplacetowork.com.
- Seramount "Best Companies" lists, https://seramount.com/best-companies/.

Pro bono

- Thomson Reuters Foundation, TrustLaw™, www.trust.org/trustlaw/.
- *Pro bono* Institute, Law Firm *Pro Bono* Project, www.probonoinst.org/projects/law-firm-pro-bono/.
- UK Collaborative Plan for *Pro Bono*, http://probonoplan.uk.
- Stanford University, Lawyers for a Sustainable Economy, https://law.stanford.edu/environmental-and-natural-resources-law-policy-program-enrlp/lawyers-for-a-sustainable-economy/.

Diversity

- Diversity Lab, Mansfield Rule: Boosting Diversity in Leadership, www.diversitylab.com/mansfield-rule-4-0/.
- The 30% Club, https://30percentclub.org/about-us/.
- Women's Empowerment Principles, www.weps.org.
- Human Rights Campaign, Best Places to Work for LGBTQ+: Equality 2022, www.hrc.org/resources/best-places-to-work-for-lgbtq-equality-2022.
- Rare Recruitment Ltd, Race Fairness Commitment, https://racefairnesscommitment.com.
- The Valuable500, www.thevaluable500.com.

Climate change

- CDP Worldwide, www.cdp.net/en/climate.
- Science Based Targets: Driving Ambitious Corporate Climate Action, https://sciencebasedtargets.org.
- United Nations Framework Convention on Climate Change, Race to Zero, https://racetozero.unfccc.int.
- ISO 14001, Environmental Management, www.iso.org/iso-14001-environmental-management.html.
- ISO 50001, Energy Management, www.iso.org/iso-50001-energy-management.html.

Supply chain

- EcoVadis, Business Sustainability Ratings, https://ecovadis.com.
- Sustainalytics, www.sustainalytics.com.
- CDP Worldwide, www.cdp.net/en/supply-chain.
- Moody's Corporation, Moody's and ESG: Advancing Global Standards, https://esg.moodys.io.

Buildings

- US Green Building Council, LEED rating system, www.usgbc.org/leed.
- Building Research Establishment, BREEAM Sustainability Assessment Method, www.breeam.com/?cn-reloaded=1.
- Alliance HQE GBC France, certifications, www.hqegbc.org/batiments/certifications/.

CSR and impact evaluation/certification

- ISO 26000 Social Responsibility, www.iso.org/iso-26000-social-responsibility.html.
- B Corporation, B Corp Certification, www.bcorporation.net/en-us/certification.

Reporting

- United Nations Global Compact, www.unglobalcompact.org. Global Reporting Initiative, www.globalreporting.org.

Notes

1 Donella H Meadows, Dennis L Meadows, Jørgen Randers and William W Behrens III, *The Limits of Growth: A Report for the Club of Rome's Project on the Predicament of Mankind*, Universe Books, 1972, www.clubofrome.org/publications/the-limits-to-growth/.
2 The IPCC is the UN body for assessing the science related to climate change. First part of the IPCC Sixth Assessment Report: "Climate Change 2021: The Physical Science Basis", www.ipcc.ch/report/sixth-assessment-report-working-group-i/.
3 Howard R Bowen, *Social Responsibilities of the Businessman*, Harper & Brothers, 1953.
4 R Edward Freeman's stakeholder theory of organisational management and business ethics is discussed in his book *Strategic Management: A Stakeholder Approach* (first edition, Pitman 1984; latest edition, Cambridge University Press 2010).
5 Adapted from Patrick d'Humières and Pierre Montel, *The Fundamentals of Sustainable Business*, CentraleSupélec Exed – Eco-Learn, 2021.
6 Directive 2014/95/EU of the European Parliament and of the Council of 22 October 2014, amending Directive 2013/34/EU as regards disclosure of non-financial and diversity information by certain large undertakings and groups, https://eur-lex.europa.eu/legal-content/EN/TXT/?uri=CELEX%3A32014L0095.
7 Rob van Tulder, *Business & The Sustainable Development Goals – A Framework for Effective Corporate Involvement*, Rotterdam School of Management/Erasmus University, 2018.
8 The tone has been set by Larry Fink, CEO of BlackRock, in his annual letters to shareholders, which since 2016 have increasingly stressed the responsibility of investors to make a positive impact on the world. In 2020, in a letter that resonated strongly in the business community, Fink discussed several commitments around climate change (eg, governance, social impact programmes, achieving net zero emissions). See Andrew Ross Sorkin, "BlackRock CEO Larry Fink: Climate Crisis Will Reshape Finance", *The New York Times*, 14 January 2020, www.nytimes.com/2020/01/14/business/dealbook/larry-fink-blackrock-climate-change.html.
9 At around the same time as Fink issued his 2020 letter to shareholders, large corporations announced impressive commitments to net zero objectives. Microsoft announced the ambitious goal of becoming carbon negative by 2030, setting a strong example to others; see Brad Smith, "One year later: The path to carbon negative – a progress report on our climate 'moonshot'", 28 January 2021, https://blogs.microsoft.com/blog/2021/01/28/one-year-later-the-path-to-carbon-negative-a-progress-report-on-our-climate-moonshot/.
10 Wayne Visser, "The Age of Responsibility: CSR 2.0 and the New DNA of Business", *Journal of Business Systems Governance and Ethics*, 5(3), October 2010, www.researchgate.net/publication/228188599_The_Age_of_Responsibility_CSR_20_and_the_New_DNA_of_Business.
11 Many law firms of all sizes and jurisdictions have an endowment fund or a foundation, such as Clifford Chance (global: www.cliffordchance.com/about_us/responsible-business/community-and-pro-bono/the-clifford-chance-foundation.html)), Delsol (France: https://delsol-lawyers.com/Endowment-fund) and Ace (Belgium: www.acelaw.be/ace-foundation), to name but a few.
12 https://legalsustainabilityalliance.com/; https://chancerylaneproject.org/; https://netzerolawyers.com/.
13 United Nations Sustainable Development Goals, www.un.org/sustainabledevelopment/sustainable-development-goals/. The content of this publication has not been approved by the United Nations and does not reflect the views of the United Nations or its officials or member states.
14 Robert G Eccles, "The Importance of the Services Sector to the Sustainable Development Goals", *Forbes*, 3 November 2019, www.forbes.com/sites/bobeccles/2019/11/03/the-importance-of-the-services-sector-to-the-sustainable-development-goals/?sh=571d6f8b78ff.
15 World Business Council for Sustainable Development, SDG Sector Roadmap Guidelines, www.wbcsd.org/Programs/People-and-Society/Sustainable-Development-Goals/SDG-Sector-Roadmaps/Resources/SDG-Sector-Roadmaps-Guidelines.
16 United Nations Sustainable Development Goals, Goal 16, www.un.org/sustainabledevelopment/peace-justice/.
17 White & Case, 2019 Global Citizenship Review, www.whitecase.com/2019-global-citizenship-review?s=2019%20Global%20Citizenship%20Review.
18 www.a4id.org/.
19 Barreau de Paris Solidarité, www.barreausolidarite.org/nos-actions/bus-solidarite.html.
20 https://chancerylaneproject.org/.
21 United Nations Sustainable Development Goals, Goal 5, www.un.org/sustainabledevelopment/gender-equality/.
22 United Nations Sustainable Development Goals, Goal 10, https://in.one.un.org/page/sustainable-development-goals/sdg-10/.
23 United Nations Sustainable Development Goals, Goal 4, www.un.org/en/academic-impact/page/quality-education.
24 InitiaDROIT, Paris Bar, www.avocatparis.org/services-de-l-ordre/initiadroit.
25 Barefoot College International, www.barefootcollege.org/.

26 UN Climate Change Conference 2021, COP26, Glasgow 31 October–12 November 2021, https://ukcop26.org.
27 Net Zero Lawyers Alliance, https://netzerolawyers.com/.
28 United Nations Sustainable Development Goals, Goal 17, www.un.org/sustainabledevelopment/globalpartnerships/.
29 Tracey Keys, Thomas W Malnight and Kees van der Graaf, "Making the most of corporate social responsibility", *McKinsey Quarterly*, 1 December 2009, www.mckinsey.com/featured-insights/leadership/making-the-most-of-corporate-social-responsibility.
30 https://netzerolawyers.com/, as expressed by Lee Ranson, chief executive of Eversheds Sutherlands International at the Alliance's launch event.
31 https://chancerylaneproject.org/.
32 Thomson Reuters Foundation, TrustLaw™, www.trust.org/trustlaw/.
33 www.dentons.com/en/about-dentons/news-events-and-awards/news/2019/september/thomson-reuters-foundation-and-nextlaw-referral-network-partner.
34 Clifford Chance, "Clifford Chance launches inaugural Sustainable Development Goals Award, targeting environmental causes", 16 August 2021, www.cliffordchance.com/news/news/2021/08/clifford-chance-launches-inaugural-sustainable-development-goals.html.
35 Hogan Lovells HLBase, www.hoganlovellsbase.com/about.
36 A quote from celebrated management consultant Peter Drucker; see, eg, The Management Centre, "Transforming results by changing beliefs and behaviours", www.managementcentre.co.uk/management-consultancy/culture-eats-strategy-for-breakfast/.
37 In Gregor Schönborn *et al*, "Why social sustainability counts: The impact of corporate social sustainability culture on financial success", *Sustainable Production and Consumption*, August 2018, www.researchgate.net/publication/327357389_Why_social_sustainability_counts_The_impact_of_corporate_social_sustainability_culture_on_financial_success.
38 Matrix adapted from Andrew Winston, "The Business Case for Sustainability", *Harvard Business Review*, 18 August 2016, www.facebook.com/HBR/videos/the-business-case-for-sustainability-with-andrew-s-winston-hbrlive/10154307869042787/.
39 INSEAD Alumni Association France, "Crisis as a catalyst of transformation: disrupt or be disrupted", *Next Normal Business Perspectives*, 28 October 2020, p10, https://blogs.insead.edu/france-iaa/publication-next-normal-business-perspectives/.
40 PACTE Law 2019-486 of 22 May 2019 on Business Growth and Transformation of Enterprises; www.legifrance.gouv.fr/jorf/id/JORFTEXT000038496102/.
41 Centaure Avocats, www.centaure-avocats.com/#raison_detre.
42 Erasmus University Rotterdam, "Driving business towards the sustainable development goals" (online course), www.coursera.org/learn/sdgbusiness.
43 Jemma Slingo, "Extinction Rebellion confirms plans to target City law firms", *The Law Society Gazette*, 24 August 2021, www.lawgazette.co.uk/news/extinction-rebellion-confirms-plans-to-target-city-law-firms/5109589.article.
44 United Nations, Department of Economic and Social Affairs, "Sustainable Development Goal 7," https://sdgs.un.org/goals/goal7.
45 Fashion United, "Global fashion industry statistics – international apparel", https://fashionunited.com/global-fashion-industry-statistics/.
46 International Labour Organization, "The Rana Plaza Accident and its aftermath", www.ilo.org/global/topics/geip/WCMS_614394/lang—en/index.htm#:~:text=On%2024%20April%202013%2C%20the%20collapse%20of%20the,Tazreen%20Fashions%20factory%20on%20the%20outskirts%20of%20Dhaka.
47 See, for example, www.imvoconvenanten.nl/en/garments-textile; https://unfashionalliance.org; and www.oecd.org/corporate/mne/responsible-supply-chains-textile-garment-sector.htm.
48 The Chancery Lane Project is a great example of lawyers assisting governments with the drafting of ESG regulations; https://chancerylaneproject.org/model-laws/.
49 Law Students for Climate Accountability, *The 2021 Law Firm Climate Change Scorecard*, www.ls4ca.org/.
50 Adam McGibbon, "Climate change activists have found the big target: mega-law firms", *Business Insider*, 24 October 2020, www.businessinsider.com/big-law-firms-climate-change-activists-strategy-pressure-politics-2020-10?IR=T.
51 IBA and Acritas, *IBA Young Lawyers' Survey*; in total, there were more than 3,000 respondents aged 40 and under, see www.ibanet.org/LPRU/Young-lawyers-survey.
52 Earlier in this special report, we identified that ESG – more than any other significant trend – reflects the various roles of law firms:

- as legal advisers for their clients;
- as business partners with an in-depth understanding of complex sectoral issues;
- as a bridge between society, policymakers and regulators and businesses; and
- as independent economic actors and part of clients' supply chains.

53 Kate Beioley, "High pay in law jobs fails to compensate for toxic culture", *Financial Times*, 14 October 2021, https://amp-ft-com.cdn.ampproject.org/c/s/amp.ft.com/content/b57dbe83-65c3-4ea7-95d1-1df878c763bd.

54 What is remarkable about this example is the firm's management of incoming work in the highly active post-pandemic period. The M&A group claims to be turning down a majority of incoming instructions relating to large one-off deals, even if they promise to be highly profitable, to avoid exhausting its workforce to the detriment of long-term clients. This is an example of a trade-off, where a brave decision is made to preserve the sustainability of the workforce and hence of the firm.
55 www.mindfulbusinesscharter.com/.
56 https://betterworkplacemh.com/.
57 IBA, *Mental Wellbeing in the Legal Profession: A Global Study*, www.ibanet.org/New-IBA-report-sets-out-principles-for-dealing-with-mental-wellbeing-crisis-in-the-legal-profession.
58 *Ibid.*
59 Quirin Schiermeier, "Eat less meat: UN climate-change report calls for change to human diet", *Nature*, 8 August 2019, www.nature.com/articles/d41586-019-02409-7.
60 Which doesn't necessarily mean that these unsustainable activities are illegal or in violation of the law.
61 Cristina Dalla Bona, "Linklaters to upskill top lawyers on ESG", *The Lawyer*, 28 July 2021, www.thelawyer.com/linklaters-to-upskill-top-lawyers-on-esg/.
62 Hogan Lovells press release, "Hogan Lovells appoints first *pro bono* partner in Europe", 5 January 2021, www.hoganlovells.com/en/news/hogan-lovells-appoints-first-pro-bono-partner-in-europe.
63 SDG 5 (Gender equality) and SDG 10 (Reduced inequalities).
64 Extensive research shows a correlation between mixed teams and performance in business. See, eg, McKinsey & Company, "Women Matter: Ten years of insight on gender diversity", 4 October 2017, www.mckinsey.com/featured-insights/gender-equality/women-matter-ten-years-of-insights-on-gender-diversity.
65 National Association of Women Lawyers, "Survey on the Promotion and Retention of Women in Law Firms", www.nawl.org/p/cm/ld/fid=2019.
66 Juristes et Associés, *La Radiographie 2020 des cabinets d'avocats d'affaires en France*, September 2020.
67 Mikaela Sabado, "Partner diversity in City 50 falls short of 30 per cent threshold", *The Lawyer*, 28 October 2021, www.thelawyer.com/partner-diversity-in-city-50-law-firms-falls-short-of-30-per-cent-threshold/?cmpid=dnews_23623838&adg=b214d023-05f4-49c9-a763-18263568ac73.
68 Conseil National des Barreaux, *"Les femmes dans la profession d'avocat: faits et chiffres"*, 1 March 2018, www.cnb.avocat.fr/fr/actualites/femmes-dans-la-profession-avocat-faits-et-chiffres.
69 See, eg, Marc Brodherson, Laura McGee and Mariana Pires dos Reis, "Women in law firms", McKinsey & Company, October 2017, www.mckinsey.com/~/media/mckinsey/featured%20insights/gender%20equality/women%20in%20law%20firms/women-in-law-firms-final-103017.pdf.
70 Venturis Consulting Group, inspired from the results of Research N°4, *Grandes Ecoles au Féminin* – 2009 and Diafora, www.grandesecolesaufeminin.fr/pdf/presentation_ipsos_gef.pdf.
71 www.droit-comme-un-h.com/.
72 Target 10.2 of the SDGs.
73 "The Speed Read: CMS's real estate reshuffle, and Clifford Chance goes Dutch", *The Lawyer*, 23 November 2018, www.thelawyer.com/the-speed-read-cmss-real-estate-reshuffle-and-clifford-chance-goes-dutch/.
74 Alex Taylor, "Eversheds to staff: You bring ideas, we'll give you bonuses", *The Lawyer*, 11 October 2017, www.thelawyer.com/eversheds-shadow-leadership-exchange-bonus/.
75 Pinsent Masons, "Pinsent Masons launches 'Spark Board' to promote inclusive decision-making", 16 September 2019, www.pinsentmasons.com/about-us/announcements/pinsent-masons-launches-spark-board.
76 In 2020 Pinsent Masons was named Most Innovative Law Firm in Europe by the *Financial Times*; www.pinsentmasons.com/about-us/announcements/most-innovative-law-firm-in-europe-by-financial-times.
77 The average pay ratio for the highest versus lowest paid employees at B corporations is 7:1 (compared to an average of 144:1); see "B Corps Doing Business Better: Narrowing the Income Gap by Reducing Pay Ratios and Uplifting Workers", B Corps, 3 March 2021, https://usca.bcorporation.net/zbtcz03z03/bcm/how-b-corps-do-business-better-narrowing-income-gap-reducing-pay-ratios-and-uplifting-workers.
78 Big Law has increasingly been appointing full-time global CSOs over the past few years, whether or not lawyers. One of the latest moves was Baker McKenzie's appointment of its first CSO partner in 2020; see Baker McKenzie, "Baker McKenzie Names Alyssa Auberger as Chief Sustainability Officer", 26 October 2020, www.bakermckenzie.com/en/newsroom/2020/10/alyssa-auberger-chief-sustainability-officer.
79 The roles of the chief development officer and the chief communications officer must be clearly and separately identified, with distinct responsibilities and agendas. Sustainability must not be understood or dealt with simply as communications or development, to avoid the risk of this being perceived as mere 'greenwashing'.
80 United Nations Climate Change, "What is the Paris Agreement?", https://unfccc.int/process-and-meetings/the-paris-agreement/the-paris-agreement.

81 Firms that set a net zero emissions objective undertake to reduce all greenhouse gas emissions, preferably based on the Greenhouse Gas (GHG) Protocol, which sets out an international framework to measure emissions as follows:
- Scope 1 emissions: Emissions for which the firm is responsible in performing its activities – whether directly (eg, from air conditioning in the buildings that they own) or indirectly (eg, from transport, such as business flights);
- Scope 2 emissions: Emissions generated by the electricity and other energy that they purchase in order to operate; and
- Scope 3 emissions: Emissions generated both upstream and downstream. While these are the hardest to calculate and are often a significant source of emissions, their disclosure is not compulsory.

82 A number of firms now apply science-based targets. They follow the recommendations of the Science Based Targets Initiative, defining their objectives based on scientific goals that are aligned with the Paris Agreement and will help to maintain global warming below 2°C or 1.5°C compared to pre-industrial temperatures. They have not only committed to reach net zero by 2050, but are also undertaking concrete steps and interim objectives to achieve this goal. They publish their undertakings in an engagement letter issued by the CEO and their objectives are certified by an independent scientific body.
83 The alliance (www.netzerolawyers.com) has set itself the following objectives to help achieve net zero:
- facilitating the decarbonisation goals both of their own organisations and of their clients;
- enhancing lawyers' capacity building and providing training; and
- promoting collaboration across the industry to achieve these goals.

The alliance invites all law firms to join and contribute to this initiative.
84 Gide, "Our new address in Paris from 1 October 2018", 28 September 2018, www.gide.com/en/news/15-rue-de-laborde-our-new-address-in-paris-from-1-october-2018.
85 The impact of employee travel when commuting to and from work is also included in scope 3 emissions and as such is of concern for law firms. More firms have thus implemented bicycle purchase schemes.
86 European Parliament, "Circular economy: definition, importance and benefits", 3 March 2021, www.europarl.europa.eu/news/en/headlines/economy/20151201STO05603/circular-economy-definition-importance-and-benefits.
87 Legal Fuel, "The paperless law office", 14 August 2018, www.legalfuel.com/the-paperless-law-office/#:~:text=Paperless%20law%20firms%20have%20the%20ability%20to%20be,the%20courthouse%2C%20or%20wherever%20your%20work%20takes%20you; Alex Hiscutt, "Seven benefits of becoming a paperless law firm", *Legal Futures*, 30 November 2021, www.legalfutures.co.uk/associate-news/seven-benefits-of-becoming-a-paperless-law-firm; Willie Peacock, "Going paperless: How to transition to a paperless law office", *Clio*, www.clio.com/blog/going-paperless-law-firm/.
88 www.fairphone.com/en/.
89 There are numerous inspiring examples of firms developing carbon sinks. For instance, in The Hague, legal executive search firm DRB ensures that 20 trees are planted through NGO Trees for All for each search completed; www.drbgroep.nl/ and https://treesforall.nl/en/.
90 EcoVadis is the world's largest provider of business sustainability ratings; https://ecovadis.com.
91 Robert F van Beemen, "International referral strategies", *Strategies for Growth in Law Firms*, Globe Law and Business, 2021, p61.
92 Alexander Osterwalder and Yves Pigneur, *Business Model Generation: A Handbook for Visionaries, Game Changers and Challengers*, Wiley, 2010.
93 Rob van Tulder, "Business and the SDGs: A Framework for Effective Corporate Involvement", Erasmus University: Rotterdam School of management 2018, p93.
94 "The SDG Compass provides guidance for companies on how they can align their strategies as well as measure and manage their contribution to the realisation of the SDGs", https://sdgcompass.org/.
95 https://sdgcompass.org/wp-content/uploads/2015/12/019104_SDG_Compass_Guide_2015.pdf.
96 ISO, Popular Standards: ISO 26000 Social Responsibility, www.iso.org/iso-26000-social-responsibility.html.
97 VIGO has more than 20 lawyers (six partners) and started its ISO journey in 2013. The firm explains that this approach is the result of continuous improvements and an ongoing process of progression; https://vigo-avocats.com/rse/.
98 The B Impact Assessment tool, https://bimpactassessment.net/.
99 See Freeman (n 4).
100 United Nations Global Compact, "The Communication on Progress (CoP) in Brief", www.unglobalcompact.org/participation/report/cop.
101 European Commission, "EU taxonomy for sustainable activities", https://ec.europa.eu/info/business-economy-euro/banking-and-finance/sustainable-finance/eu-taxonomy-sustainable-activities_en.
102 www.globalreporting.org/.
103 White & Case, "2019 Global Citizenship Review", www.whitecase.com/2019-global-citizenship-review?s=2019%20Global%20Citizenship%20Review.
104 Clifford Chance, "Reports, data and insights", www.cliffordchance.com/about_us/responsible-business/reports-data-and-insights.html.

105 Science Based Targets, "SBTi launches world-first net-zero corporate standard", 28 October 2021, https://sciencebasedtargets.org/news/sbti-launches-world-first-net-zero-corporate-standard.
106 United Nations Global Compact, "The Communication on Progress (CoP) in Brief", www.unglobalcompact.org/participation/report/cop.
107 Global Reporting Initiative, www.globalreporting.org/.
108 See, eg, Tim Quinson, "Regulators Intensify ESG Scrutiny as Greenwashing Explodes", *Bloomberg Green*, 1 September 2021, www.bloomberg.com/news/articles/2021-09-01/regulatory-scrutiny-of-esg-greenwashing-is-intensifying.
109 European Commission, "Delivering the European Green Deal", https://ec.europa.eu/info/strategy/priorities-2019-2024/european-green-deal/delivering-european-green-deal_en.
110 Hague District Court, *Milieudefensie v Royal Dutch Shell plc* (C/09/571932 / HA ZA 19-379), https://uitspraken.rechtspraak.nl/inziendocument?id=ECLI:NL:RBDHA:2021:5339&showbutton=true &keyword=shell.
111 Netflix, "'Breaking boundaries': The road to a cleaner, healthier and more peaceful world", 22 April 2021, https://about.netflix.com/en/news/breaking-boundaries-the-science-of-our-planet.
112 Kat Kramer and Joe Ware, "Counting the cost of 2021: A year of climate breakdown", Christian Aid, December 2021, www.christianaid.org.uk/sites/default/files/2021-12/Counting%20the%20cost%202021%20-%20A%20year%20of%20climate%20breakdown.pdf.
113 The tragedy of the commons is an economics problem in which every individual has an incentive to consume a resource, but at the expense of every other individual, with no way of excluding others from consumption. Initially, it was formulated by asking what would happen if all shepherds, acting in their own self-interest, allowed their flocks to graze on a common field. If everybody acted in their apparent own best interest, it would result in harmful overconsumption (all the grass would be eaten, to the detriment of all) (Source: Investopedia, Tragedy of the commons, 23 October 2020, www.investopedia.com/terms/t/tragedy-of-the-commons.asp).
114 https://wikitia.com/wiki/Mansfield_Rule.

About the authors

Robert F van Beemen
Partner, Dicke Röell Breedveld
vanbeemen@drbgroep.nl

Robert F van Beemen is a partner at Dicke Röell Breedveld, a legal executive search, coaching and strategy firm in the Netherlands. His main focus is advising boutique and national independent law firms in the Benelux on market positioning, strategic reviews, ESG and international strategy formulation, and strategic business planning.

He started his career in 2007 as a corporate and restructuring lawyer with a large Dutch Caribbean law firm in Curaçao. From 2014 to May 2022 Robert was a partner at Venturis Consulting Group.

Robert holds an LLM in corporate law and is an alumnus of the Rotterdam School of Management, Erasmus University. He is an officer of the International Bar Association Law Firm Management Committee (including the ESG working group) and an active member of the International Association of Young Lawyers (AIJA). He regularly publishes and speaks about ESG, international developments and the impact on the strategies and business models of law firms.

Sophie Boyer Chammard
Partner, Venturis Consulting Group
sophie.boyer.chammard@venturisconsulting.com

Sophie Boyer Chammard, a Paris-based partner at Venturis Consulting Group, has been active in the legal market for more than 25 years.

Sophie advises law firms on profitable and sustainable revenue growth strategies, and helps them to design client-centred development strategies. She accompanies firms that wish to improve their positive impact – whether social, societal and/or environmental – and include their responsibility as a core element in their profitable growth strategy.

She builds on eight years' experience as a finance and M&A lawyer, and 20 years as a strategy and business development professional, both at law firms (Clifford Chance, Gide and Hogan Lovells) and as a strategy consultant (at Andersen Consulting and independently).

Sophie holds an MBA from INSEAD, an LLB in English and French law from King's College London and a master's in business and tax law from the Sorbonne Paris I.

About Globe Law and Business

Globe Law and Business was established in 2005. From the very beginning, we set out to create law books which are sufficiently high level to be of real use to the experienced professional, yet still accessible and easy to navigate. Most of our authors are drawn from Magic Circle and other top commercial firms, both in the UK and internationally.

Our titles are carefully produced, with the utmost attention paid to editorial, design and production processes. We hope this results in high-quality publications that are easy to read, and a pleasure to own. Our titles are also available as ebooks, which are compatible with most desktop, laptop and tablet devices. In 2018 we expanded our portfolio to include journals and Special Reports, available both digitally and in hard copy format, and produced to the same high standards as our books.

In the spring of 2021, we were very pleased to announce the start of a new chapter for Globe Law and Business following the acquisition of law books under the imprint Ark Publishing. We are very much looking forward to working with our Ark authors, many of whom are well known to us, to further developing the law firm management list, and to welcoming our new Ark customers.

We'd very much like to hear from you with your thoughts and ideas for improving what we offer. Please do feel free to email me at sian@globelawandbusiness.com with your views.

Sian O'Neill
Managing director
Globe Law and Business
www.globelawandbusiness.com

www.ingramcontent.com/pod-product-compliance
Ingram Content Group UK Ltd.
Pitfield, Milton Keynes, MK11 3LW, UK
UKHW051203081125
464838UK00006B/46